OUR EARLY ANCESTORS

RECONSTRUCTED VIEW OF PILE DWELLING AND VILLAGE

OUR EARLY ANCESTORS

AN INTRODUCTORY STUDY OF MESOLITHIC, NEOLITHIC AND COPPER AGE CULTURES IN EUROPE AND ADJACENT REGIONS

by

M. C. BURKITT, M.A., F.S.A., F.G.S.

University Lecturer at Cambridge in the Faculty of Archaeology and Anthropology.
Author of Prehistory, Our Forerunners, South Africa's Past in Stone
and Paint, *etc.*

CAMBRIDGE
AT THE UNIVERSITY PRESS
MCMXXIX

CAMBRIDGE UNIVERSITY PRESS
Cambridge, New York, Melbourne, Madrid, Cape Town,
Singapore, São Paulo, Delhi, Tokyo, Mexico City

Cambridge University Press
The Edinburgh Building, Cambridge CB2 8RU, UK

Published in the United States of America by Cambridge University Press, New York

www.cambridge.org
Information on this title: www.cambridge.org/9781107694071

First published 1926
Reprinted 1929
First paperback edition 2011

A catalogue record for this publication is available from the British Library

ISBN 978-1-107-69407-1 Paperback

PREFACE

It is far easier to write a text-book on Palaeolithic than on Neolithic times. Just as the average geologist will readily sketch out a clear and comprehensive account of Palaeozoic times, but may fail to derive any consistent story from Quaternary gravels and other late deposits, so the prehistorian finds the earlier Palaeolithic cultures much easier to deal with, than the far more complicated, though later and more fully preserved, Neolithic and early Metal Age remains. The difficulties are of three kinds. Firstly, where so much has been preserved for us to study, a far more detailed and wider knowledge is required, and this is for the most part only gained by actual work in the field or prolonged study in many a foreign museum. Published results are generally to be found scattered through numberless papers and journals, many of them local publications not always easy to come across. Secondly, having acquired a certain number of facts, the writer has to settle what he is going to leave out, and this is by no means his lightest task. The following book, as the title states, is meant to act as an introduction to the study of the Mesolithic, Neolithic, and earliest Metal Ages and, as such, details of purely local significance are naturally out of place. The writer in the course of lecturing has felt the lack of such a book and, although he is painfully aware of the shortcomings of the present volume, he feels that such an introductory text-book may be welcome to many a student who, with the help of the bibliographies, will afterwards be able to proceed further either in the elucidation of the industries of a given area or in some more general problem. Curiously enough very few text-books, covering the periods in question, have been published, but among serious works are *The Cambridge Ancient History*, vol. I, and V. G. Childe's *The Dawn of European Civilisation*, a book that no student of the subject can afford to leave unstudied, though brilliant as it is with its wealth of detail, a certain knowledge of typology is unavoidably assumed. Thirdly there is the difficulty that confronts the writer of such a book as this, namely the choice of a method of approach. Naturally the area to be considered has first to be decided upon, the whole world cannot be covered in a single work. But humanity is so interrelated and outside influences from far-off districts have all so played their part in the building up of European Neolithic and early Metal Age cultures that it is not easy to know where to draw the line. Again, should a geographical or a chronological scheme be followed? If the former the pre-history of many areas must be followed separately, and a number of histories produced, consistent in themselves but not always easy to interrelate, while the interaction of all the different cultures makes the second method one of great difficulty. However one may expect in the future that still more importance will be attached to making and utilising distribution maps, in which all finds of a given industry are carefully plotted out on an ordinary large scale map with the result that the exact limits of a given industry or culture, and sometimes its movements and interactions, can be determined. This long and painstaking work is far from completion, even as far as Europe is concerned, and it will be many years before the work, which requires detailed knowledge of every find both ancient and modern, is in any sense finished.

My most sincere thanks are due to many kind friends for help in the compilation of the present work. Firstly I want to thank my wife who has not only helped materially in the text itself, but has also drawn all the plates that were not directly reproduced from other works, except the map, for which I am indebted to my father. Mr V. Gordon Childe has been most kind in making suggestions and criticisms. Dr Haddon, always a tower of strength to the would-be author has, as always, been more than kind and helpful. Miss Askwith and Mrs Quiggin have relieved me of all the mechanical troubles connected with its production, not to speak of the index making. I also desire to thank my aunt, Miss Parry, who has taken upon herself the correcting of the proof-sheets. Several colleagues have most kindly allowed me to copy illustrations from their published works; to Dr F. Johannsen, Dr Reinerth, Dr Åberg and Mr F. Buckley I am especially indebted in this respect. The figures of implements in chapter IV are mostly drawn from originals in the Cambridge Museum of Archaeology and Ethnology or in my own collection. A number of references to a small bibliography appear at the end of each chapter. Certain works of especial importance to the student are marked with an asterisk.

M. C. BURKITT

Cambridge, 1926

CONTENTS

ILLUSTRATIONS

The frontispiece is reproduced from *The New Stone Age in Northern Europe*, by permission of Messrs Charles Scribner's Sons, New York, and G. Bell & Sons, Ltd., London.

OUR EARLY ANCESTORS

INTRODUCTION

THE history of mankind—like the journals or proceedings of many learned societies—has been divided into several volumes, each of which comprises a number of separate parts. The third, and still unfinished, volume of mankind's history is concerned with the so-called Iron Age which begins when this metal came into common use for tool-making and other general purposes. The second volume contains the history of an earlier epoch before the smelting of iron ores had been properly discovered, and when copper and its alloy with tin—bronze—were the only metals usually employed for tool-making, although gold, silver and lead occur and were sometimes worked up into objects of ornament, etc. The history and conditions of human existence in this, the earlier, age of metal, is one of surpassing interest and already very complex. Whether we turn our eyes to the wonderful palaces and towns of Bronze Age Crete, Greece, and the Aegean generally, with their wealth of gold objects and artistically painted pots, faience figures, wall paintings, etc., or to the important trade routes that first sprang up at this time across northern Europe, enabling the highly prized Baltic amber to be conveyed up the valleys and over the passes to the more settled and developed Mediterranean lands, we cannot fail to be astonished at the modernity of these early cultures. Of course nature had not yet been harnessed to the service of man to the same extent as she is to-day, but after all, on analysis, this harnessing of nature can, to a very large extent, be expressed in the word *transport*. To-day we transport ourselves and our goods in trains and steamships, and our thoughts and words by telegraphs, telephones and wireless. Although Bronze Age Crete had no broadcasting, the germs of much of our modern civilisation can be already discerned. Beyond the Alps, in spite of the fact that trade routes were springing up, and an interchange of commerce and culture with the south was growing, the cultures of the northern lands lagged behind those of the Mediterranean basin, and there is nothing comparable to the brilliance of the south. Wealth there was in abundance in the shape of gold, as can be seen to-day by anyone who delves into the vaults of the National Museum at Budapest, but the art, decoration and workmanship remain barbaric, and there is nothing corresponding to the delicacy and skilful design of such objects as the cups from Vaphio in Laconia with their embossed scenes of the wild ox being caught in a net and then, tamed, being led by a foot rope.

The history of mankind that Volume 1 lays before us is very different. Here we find no knowledge of metals manifested; all tools were made of wood, bone, or stone; moreover, during the earlier and far longer portion of this period (corresponding in our "proceedings" analogy to Parts 1, 2, 3, 4 and 5, out of a total of 6), there was no knowledge of agriculture or pottery, and animals had not yet been domesticated. Mankind—in Europe and the Mediterranean basin, the area mainly under review in this little book—was still in the hunting stage; and, in spite of the existence of a wonderful art practised for magic purposes by the folk of the Later Old Stone Age—an art that, given the circumstances, we should have a difficulty in rivalling to-day—it must be admitted that during most of the time included in Volume 1 humanity was in a very different and more primitive state of culture than exists in Europe to-day, and that the germs of our modern civilisation are not much in evidence.

At this point it will be convenient to give a table showing in a simplified manner the various sub-divisions of the history of mankind.

Volume III, part 3 = Steel Age.
           part 2 = Newer Iron Age or La Tène Culture.
           part 1 = Older Iron Age or Hallstatt Culture.
Volume II, part 3 = Later Bronze Age.
           part 2 = Earlier Bronze Age.
           part 1 = Copper Age (Eneolithic or Chalcolithic Culture).
Volume I,   part 6 = Neolithic Period.
           part 5 = Mesolithic Period.
           part 4 = Upper Palaeolithic Period.
           part 3 = Middle Palaeolithic Period.
           part 2 = Lower Palaeolithic Period.
           part 1 = Eolithic Period.

Our concern in this book is with Volume I, parts 5 and 6, and Volume II, part 1, but naturally a word or two must be said of the cultures just preceding and just following in order that our particular period may be satisfactorily placed in its proper sequence and thus be duly realised in relation to both its background and foreground.

The older prehistorians did not admit the Mesolithic Period as a separate entity. For them there was the Palaeolithic, grouped as in our table, but including the earlier part of what we have classed as Mesolithic, while the later part of this same period was grouped as Early Neolithic. The criteria employed to determine whether a given industry on the border line should be classed as Palaeolithic or Neolithic were: (1) the presence or absence of pottery, (2) the presence or absence of evidence for domestic animals and agriculture, (3) whether polishing and grinding were employed in the making of tools, or merely chipping. It is now recognised, however, that these criteria alone lead to anomalies. The two contemporary folk who have left us heaps of their kitchen refuse, the one on the shores of the Baltic and the other in North Spain, and who, in spite of many differences, are in many ways very similar in culture, would, under the old scheme, have to be completely separated, the former being classed as Early Neolithic, the latter as Late Palaeolithic. At the end of Upper Palaeolithic times a rapid change of temperature took place in Western Europe and the climate ameliorated, and with this change of climate the Palaeolithic history of mankind closed. On the other hand we cannot class everything after this change as Neolithic, for during a long period mankind was living a very different life from that of the true New Stone Age. It is therefore convenient to create this Mesolithic stage to include all those industries and cultures yet but dimly known that start at the end of Magdalenian times on the change of climate and finish with the appearance in quantity, in western and northern Europe, of the polished stone celts and the megalithic tombs. Although the Old Stone Age hunter was no doubt largely exterminated or, at any rate, became extinct with the change of climate and conditions, a remnant probably survived throughout Mesolithic times and even influenced the higher culture of the New Stone Age invader before becoming finally absorbed into the new civilisation. How great an influence this Old Stone Age element had in moulding the history of the newer folk it is difficult to say with any degree of certainty. There have been some students of the subject, however, who see the influence of the older cave burials in the desire to build the large megalithic tombs which are so frequently found in the so-called Western and Northern Neolithic Areas.

To paint in our background it will not be necessary to summarise the whole of Palaeolithic times; those who are interested in this dim past have many works, both large and small, to consult(1), but a brief picture of the life and times of Upper Palaeolithic folk (Volume 1, part 4, of our table) will not be out of place.

The roots of Palaeolithic study are to a great extent firmly fixed in geological history, and we must therefore start by seeing what the Quaternary geologists can tell us as to the climate, conditions and fauna that the Upper Palaeolithic hunter had to contend with. If readers could be borne back through the ages in Titania's car and landed in France during Palaeolithic times, they would find the situation very different from that which obtains to-day. During most of the time under review cold, dry, steppe conditions prevailed, except near mountain masses like the Alps, where ice-fields and long glaciers penetrating far into the plains produced tundra conditions. There were short hot summers, it is true, but these were no compensation for the long cruel winters. The Upper Palaeolithic hunter and his family lived on the sunny side of valleys, under overhanging rocks or in the mouths of caves. It is not true to say that he actually lived in the depths of the caves themselves, for his industries, the cinders of his fires and so on, are never found in these places. Nor should we expect it; the interiors of caves are not only absolutely dark, requiring artificial light continually, but are also often very damp, and rheumatism was apparently not unknown even in that remote past.

Again, it would be unsatisfactory to have left your family in the depth of a cave, while necessary hunting for food took place, and to return to find that a cave bear had taken up his residence in the vestibule! Food consisted of game, which included many animals extinct to-day, such as the mammoth and the woolly rhinoceros, and others which no longer exist under the warmer skies of our western Europe, such as the reindeer and the bison. The objects found in the "homes" include flint scrapers, graving tools, awls, etc., antler harpoons, lance points and needles. These latter are often small, beautifully made and eyed, and were no doubt employed in the sewing together of small skins for the purpose of making clothes. Objects of art are common in the latter part of this period, and paintings and engravings have been found in the depths of caves. These caves, however, seem to have been of the nature of temples, and this art seems to have been a sympathetic magic to help the food supply(a). The cave home was kept warm by the fires at which the food was cooked, and no doubt a rude degree of comfort was obtainable. Cups for drinking purposes, in the form of carefully shaped pieces of skull, have been discovered, as well as necklaces made from animals' teeth or shells—these being sometimes sea-shells brought, in more than one instance, from as far as sixty miles away. Careful ceremonial burial was often practised.

The population of such a country as France must in those days have been very small. A land, under the best conditions, only supports a small hunting population, and the climate in those days did not provide the best conditions.

Then all at once, due to unknown causes, everything changed. The climate suddenly ameliorated, the old fauna and flora vanished, and with them went the old hunter; the last page of part 4 is closed and we turn next to part 5.

BIBLIOGRAPHY AND REFERENCES

(1) See, for example, *Fossil Man in Spain*, by Dr H. Obermaier; *Ancient Hunters*, by W. J. Sollas; *Men of the Old Stone Age*, by H. F. Osborn; *Prehistory* and *Our Forerunners*, by M. C. Burkitt (Home University Series).

(2) M. C. BURKITT, *Our Forerunners* (Home University Series). Chapters 9 and 10.

CHAPTER I

MESOLITHIC TIMES

THE problem of the Transition Period lying between the series of cultures that are grouped together as Palaeolithic and the Neolithic civilisation, and which is often named the Mesolithic Period, has long occupied the attention of the prehistorian investigator. Formerly nothing was known of the many industries that characterise this Mesolithic Period, and the investigator found himself face to face with an apparently catastrophic change in everything at the end of Palaeolithic times, when the old industries and fauna and wonderful art all suddenly disappear, their place being taken by the, it must be admitted, dreary industries and cultures of early post-Palaeolithic times. The hiatus between the Old and the New Stone Ages seemed to be so marked that for a long time it was considered that at the close of the Quaternary Period Europe became desolate and uninhabited, until, at a much later date, fresh invasions, from the east, of New Stone Age folk, repopulated the continent. Towards the end of the nineteenth century Piette, a French prehistorian and one of the pioneers of the subject, started digging operations in the cave of Mas d'Azil (Ariège, France). The situation of this cave is remarkable: the River Arise flowing down a shallow valley suddenly turns to the left and plunges through a low limestone range. The tunnel so formed, which is about a quarter of a mile in length, is large enough to be utilised to-day for the main road which runs alongside the river. Half way through further caves open on the right-hand side, looking down stream. They are of very great extent, and it is said that at the time of the Albigensian Wars an army took refuge in them and was completely concealed. At their junction with the main tunnel rich Upper Palaeolithic deposits of the Magdalenian Period had already been discovered, but it was on the left bank of the river (always looking down stream) where it enters the hill, that Piette commenced digging operations and the following succession of deposits was observed[1]:

> Surface soil.
> Neolithic: Bronze (with foundry).
> Loam with new industry = Azilian.
> Sterile loam with reindeer bones.
> Black loam with reindeer bones and Magdalenian industries similar to those of the right bank. See above.
> Sterile gravels.

From this section it will be seen that a new industry lying between the Neolithic and Bronze cultures on the one hand and the Late Magdalenian on the other had been demonstrated, and for a time it seemed as if the old problem of a hiatus had been solved and the Transition culture connecting the two found. Later investigation, however, showed that this was only partly true. This new Azilian culture was found to have only a limited distribution, and it has been shown that in Europe alone there are certainly four different cultures of Transitional date that, under the old classification, would still have to be considered as Palaeolithic. As has been said before, the modern Mesolithic section comprises also what used to be classed as Early Neolithic cultures because something was known about pottery and domestic animals, etc. But, as will be seen, they are very different from the cultures of the true Neolithic folk, and have close connections with those of the earlier Transitional peoples. The Mesolithic Period includes the following cultures:

1. Azilian.   4. Maglemosean.
2. Tardenoisean.   5. Kitchen Midden.
3. Asturian.   6. Campignian.

(N.B. No chronological sequence is indicated by this table of cultures.)

AZILIAN CULTURE

This was the first Transitional culture discovered. The climate and conditions under which the folk lived were not so very different from those of to-day, although, judging from the quantity of snail shells found in the excavations in South France, it was at any rate there rather damper. Forests probably abounded. The fauna also was not dissimilar and the Quaternary animals had disappeared. With the exception of dogs found in Azilian excavations at La Tourasse (Pyrenees) and at Oban (a) domesticated animals are absent. In place of the splendid bone tools and beautifully made, if monotonous, flint work of Magdalenian times, the industries consist of bone polishers, spatulae or chisels, rough bone awls and poorly made flint tools, including especially a large number of small round scrapers. A new type of harpoon occurs, broader and flatter than that made by Magdalenian man and with poorly cut barbs cut into, rather than projecting from, the line of the edge (Plate 1, fig. 1, *a*, *b*). As a rule the material is stag's antler; reindeer, exclusively used by the older folk for this purpose, being very rare. A hole for attachment to a haft is common, taking the form of a round or more often almond-shaped splayed hole through the base of the stem. With the old Palaeolithic hunter went his wondrous art, and in

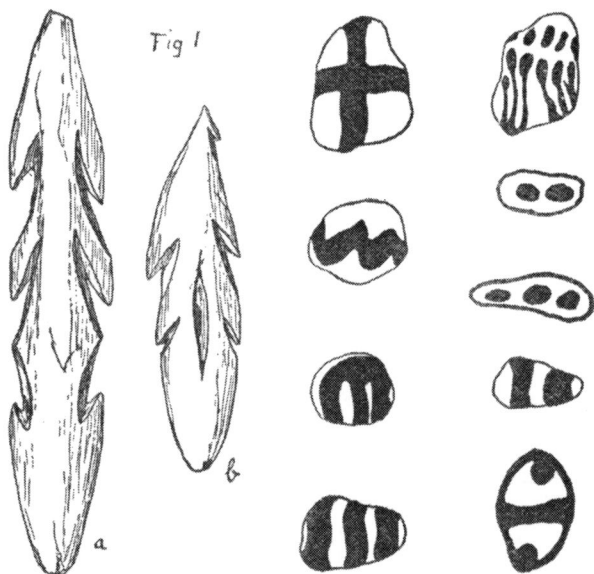

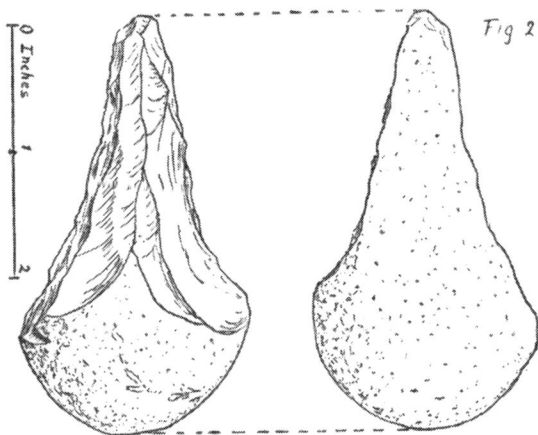

Plate 1, fig. 1. Azilian harpoons (scale about ⅔) and examples of "painted pebbles." Plate 1, fig. 2. A typical Asturian pick.

Azilian deposits we no longer find decorated bones, tools and harpoons. Only one engraved object of Azilian date is known, and this merely consists of a stone covered with meaningless engraved lines. On the other hand the so-called "painted pebbles" occur (Plate 1, fig. 1). These consist of river pebbles, rounded and smoothed by natural water action, that had been collected and smeared over with red ochre in the form of dots, bars, wavy lines, or combinations of these. The pebbles, consisting as they do for the most part of hard quartzite, have not absorbed the ochre paint which remains on the surface and can be removed altogether by slight friction. That they belong to this period is shown by their being found in Azilian deposits associated with the harpoon and other tools, and, in one case at any rate, being encrusted with stalagmitic deposits that have accumulated in the Azilian layer owing to the dampness of the cave. Their distribution is not quite as wide as the Azilian culture itself; they are not a *sine qua non* in Azilian industries, but they have been found in North Spain, the Pyrenees, and East France, etc., up to just south of Basle[1]. The motive for painting these river pebbles and their use is unknown. Dr Obermaier suggests that in some cases, at any rate, the paintings are meant to represent conventionalised human forms. This idea arises from a suggested analogy with undoubted conventionalisations of human beings found in rock shelters which belong to the Copper Age art of Spanish Art Group III, to be described in chapter x. It is however a little difficult to connect the two. There is a consider-

[1] So-called Azilian "painted pebbles" were long ago discovered in the precincts of Late Celtic brochs in Caithness and published tentatively as such. Later writers have copied this tentative suggestion as fact. An examination of the specimens themselves at once disproves this contention.

able difference in time between them, not to speak of culture. It has been suggested that these painted pebbles were of the nature of money, counting boards, talismans, etc., but none of these explanations seems to fit the case satisfactorily. In one place all the painted pebbles were found to be carefully broken in two (whether by friend or foe is of course unknown); this would seem to indicate that they were objects of some considerable importance there. It has been suggested that they were only playthings, and there is no particular reason why this explanation should be much less likely than any of the others. Certain cave paintings, shown by their superposition to be later than the last phase of Magdalenian art, which consist of barbed lines, etc., there being no animal figures or the like, have been considered to be Azilian in date, also a few conventionalised human figures, such as the two little men in the vestibule at Castillo (3); but of this there is no proof. It is still uncertain whether any of the art found in rock shelters in Spain south of the northern mountains is Azilian.

The distribution of Azilian industries, using the flat harpoon above described as the "type fossil," is important. They have been found in: North Spain as far west as Asturias[1]; the central districts of the French Pyrenees; East France(4); Switzerland, just southwards of Basle(5); Belgium, near Liège; Britain, at Victoria Cave near Settle, western Yorkshire (Plate 1, fig. 1, *b*), near Kirkcudbright, at Oban (Argyll) in, at least, two sites—McArthur's Cave and Drumvaig[2], on Oronsay Island, and elsewhere.

The cradle of this culture is not yet very clearly

[1] Probably the culture will also turn up in Galicia, though it has not yet been noted in Portugal.

[2] The finds from these places are in the Museum at Edinburgh.

known and will be considered in conjunction with the next or Tardenoisean culture. It would seem, however, that Azilian influence was felt by the Late Magdalenian folk of the Pyrenees before it had reached the Dordogne. In other words, Azilian culture either arrived in western Europe from the south, i.e. Spain, south of the Pyrenees, or possibly from the south-east. Difficulties arise because there is as yet so little evidence for the occurrence of Azilian cultures in Spain south of the Pyrenees or south of the Cordillera Cantabrica which really form an extension of the Pyrenees. Again, eastwards, the mouths of the Rhône and the flood lands around must have proved a barrier that could not have been easily crossed much lower than the latitude of Nîmes without rafts or canoes, and of these there is no evidence in Azilian times unless we allow that the English Channel had by now been formed, in which case the British Azilian folk must have arrived in our country by boat. All the same, if a culture did cross the Rhône somewhere about where the lowest railway bridge over the river exists to-day, it would still reach the Pyrenees before the Dordogne, which is separated from the Rhône valley by the whole massif of the central highlands of France.

TARDENOISEAN CULTURE

The Tardenoisean culture introduces a very different state of affairs. The Azilians, for the most part, lived in the mouths of caves or in rock shelters, and we generally find a definite stratigraphy with deposits containing Palaeolithic industries. But in the case of the Tardenoisean deposits there is seldom such clear and definite stratigraphical sequence. The industries are for the most part found on or close to the surface, except at a few sites, as for example at Zonhoven and at the cave

Remouchamps(6), both in Belgium. The industries consist of pigmy flints, generally chipped to form geometrical shapes such as the triangle—equilateral, isosceles or scalene—little crescents or lunates, and, at a slightly later date, though not in true Tardenoisean industries, trapezes (Plate 2, fig. 1). The small pigmy burin is also common, and it may be remarked that, though its absence from an industry does not disprove a Tardenoisean culture, its presence makes it almost certain[1].

As regards the chipping of most of these pigmy flints it should be noted that it consists in the blunting of the edge by the removal of small flakes rather than in the sharpening of it. The working edge of a tool was the sharp natural flake cutting-edge which is left untrimmed for use in the completed tool.

Pigmy industries have a very wide distribution, and in their connection a word of warning must be sounded. What happened was that mankind discovered the advantages of a composite tool, that is a tool composed of several elements each of which have their special useful properties. A flint flake is very sharp and very suitable for a knife blade or saw tooth, but is very brittle. The combination, however, of a wooden or bone haft into which little pigmy flakes are fixed to form either a

---

[1] The term burin or graving tool is perhaps rather a misnomer, as it is hardly conceivable that this minute tool, sometimes not a centimetre in length, had much to do with engraving. The fact to emphasise, however, is the occurrence of the highly specialised and peculiar "burin technique" so common in Upper Palaeolithic times, which has here survived and which consists of the removing of a small facet, known as the burin facet, more or less along a side of the tiny flake, starting at the working edge, a blow being delivered vertically, the flake being also held vertically. In the case of trimming and most other forms of flint chipping the blow is delivered vertically but the object is held horizontally (Plate 23, *b, c, i, n, q, b*[1]).

continuous knife blade or, in the form of irregular teeth, a kind of saw, is very serviceable. Such a discovery may have been made at different times in different parts of the world. But it should be noted that for a composite tool only certain shapes of little pigmy flakes are convenient. A carefully formed square of flint or a circle would be singularly useless, while the practical properties of a triangle with one side blunted for convenience of hafting as shown on page 34 (the blunting preventing the flake being driven too far into the haft and so splitting it) can be readily appreciated. Little flakes hafted along the lengths of bone stems have actually been found in the peat bogs in Denmark, belonging to another and doubtless contemporary Transitional culture. The occurrence, then, in different sites, of pigmy industries does not denote either a similarity of culture with that of the Tardenoisean of Europe and the Mediterranean basin, nor, of course, contemporaneity. Quite conceivably the pigmy industries near by in Poland or Southern Russia may belong to this Tardenoisean culture, but there is no proof as yet adduced to show that similar pigmy industries south of the Panjab in India, or others in Australia, or elsewhere in far distant lands, have any connection whatever with the Transitional culture we are describing, or that they are anywhere near this culture in date (Plate 2, fig. 2). In the special case of the Obsidian industry found in the district east of the Victoria Nyanza and near Lake Naivasha (Africa), where scrapers, knife blades, pigmies, etc., occur, the above argument does not apply as the burin—absent in India and Australia—is frequently found. The age of this industry must be Transitional or even Late Palaeolithic.

Tardenoisean industries are found at one site in the cave of Valle near Gibaja[7] (a station on the railway line

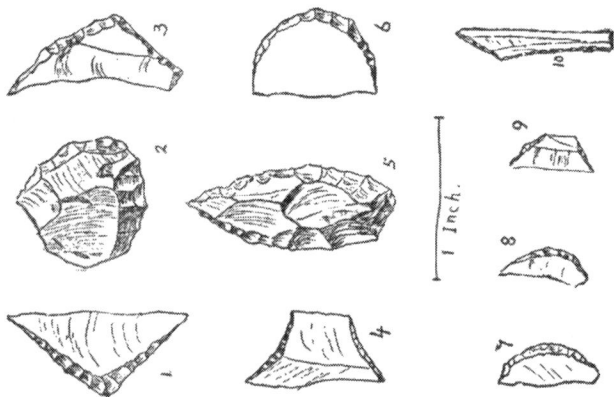

Plate 2, fig. 2. Small industries from far-off countries. 1–6 Australia, 7 Ceylon, 8–10 India.

Plate 2, fig. 1. Tardenoisean pigmies from France, Belgium, Portugal, and the Mediterranean basin.

from Bilbao to Santander, Spain) associated with little round scrapers and other Azilian tools including the harpoon. This fact is important as showing the contemporaneity of the Azilian and Tardenoisean industries. In view of the fact that the Tardenoisean has a much wider distribution than the Azilian, although of the same age, it is convenient for many purposes to group the two together and to talk of an Azilio-Tardenoisean culture.

The distribution of the Tardenoisean culture is important. It seems to be especially concentrated around the Mediterranean basin, but westward of the Alpine ranges it spreads sporadically as far north as England, and eastwards it is found in the Crimea[22], in Poland at Assowka[19], etc. and in the south of Russia. At Termini Imerese[8] in Sicily there has been found a series of tools, apparently much more recent than those of undoubted Upper Palaeolithic (Aurignacian) culture which occur in the cave of Romanelli (Otranto) and other places. These Termini Imerese industries are very similar to those found in the upper beds at the Grotte des Enfants, Mentone, which we shall have to consider in connection with the origin of the Azilio-Tardenoisean culture as a whole. The same sort of thing is found in Syria and in North Africa, where the last Capsian (that is the African Aurignacian) shows a decrease in the number of graving tools but a big increase in geometric microliths, which, although not especially Azilian in appearance, are typically Tardenoisean. Various sites in Portugal and in both North and South Spain[1] have yielded typical Tardenoisean industries. In Belgium[9] two well-defined geometric microlithic industries have been observed at

---

[1] It is interesting to note that in a rock shelter near Alpera, covered with paintings both in the Spanish Art Group II and III styles, was found a typical geometric-shaped tool.

Zonhoven; the first comes from some depth below the surface soil, the other from the surface. The former has not been intermixed with outside material and comprises long and round scrapers, gravers, microlith knife blades and little triangles. The surface industry includes Neolithic arrow heads and a flint blade the flint of which must have come from Grand Pressigny, as well as polished Neolithic axes of a late type. Associated with these are late Tardenoisean types including the trapeze. The Belgian cave of Remouchamps (6) has yielded small round scrapers, gravers and long microliths. Reindeer bones occur and trapezes are absent. In our own country a typical Transitional industry is found in North Cornwall and microliths with the burin are found at Hastings. On the Pennines near Huddersfield (10)[1] rich finds, showing Belgian connections as well as local variations, have been collected. Pigmy tools occur elsewhere at many sites, but the absence of typical implements, especially of the Tardenoisean burin, precludes any certainty as to the culture—e.g. the pigmy industries from most of the Sussex sites, etc.

The origin of the Azilio-Tardenoisean is well seen at the cave called the Grotte des Enfants near Mentone (11). Here rich Upper Palaeolithic (Aurignacian) deposits have been found undisturbed by the Solutrean and Magdalenian phases occurring elsewhere. The Aurignacian folk seem to have developed on their own lines, and their fauna shows us that they existed under the various changes of climate that elsewhere in France coincided with the coming of the Solutreans and the occurrence of the Magdalenian cultures. This Aurignacian culture at Mentone continued its development

[1] See chapter VII and Plate 23 for an account of these English pigmy industries.

undisturbed, and as we observe the evolution of the shouldered points we note how they get smaller and smaller, how the scrapers get tinier and tinier, until in the upper levels we suddenly realise that we are in the presence of true Azilio-Tardenoisean industries though without the harpoon, the source and original form of which is unknown. In other words, there seems very little doubt that the Azilio-Tardenoisean Transitional culture as a whole was developed in Europe by the old Aurignacian (Neoanthropic) stock. The original Aurignacian invader of Europe underwent many modifications, as is attested by the considerable differences that exist in the skeleton form in various times. Azilio-Tardenoisean man seems then to be a modification of this old stock that took place at the change of climate, more especially around the Mediterranean coasts, a stock that continued to survive, undergoing many further modifications caused by the pressure of the oncoming Neolithic civilisation, until it finally went under and Europe passed definitely under the sway of the New Stone Age.

As in the case of the Azilian culture so in that of the Tardenoisean nothing has been noted in the way of art, there are not even such unsatisfying objects as the "painted pebbles"!

Accounts of several careful burials of peculiar interest belonging to the Azilio-Tardenoisean culture have been published. One of the most important of these is a cave burial at Ofnet in Bavaria(12). The section in the cave shows fallen blocks at the base with dolomitic sand lying about them; on this sand rests an Aurignacian layer, then a Solutrean and then an Upper Magdalenian; on this latter is found an Azilian layer, which in turn is covered with Neolithic and recent deposits.

Here two shallow pits or nests that penetrated into, but of course had nothing to do with, the underlying Magdalenian layer had been excavated in Azilian times. In these pits or nests a number of human skulls were found buried with ochre, but without any trace of the skeletons that belonged to them. In fact, when the base of the skulls is carefully examined scratchings and cut lines can be observed, indicating a carefully executed decapitation. The skulls were deposited in these shallow pits or nests in concentric circles all facing towards the setting sun. One nest contained as many as twenty-seven skulls. The heads were those of old women, young women and young men; it is stated that as a general rule the heads of the old women had associated with them many more necklaces and other objects of ornament than those of the young women, while the men had none. In one case, that of a child, with the skull were found hundreds of shells all placed very close together perhaps by some grieving parent. The associated industries comprise Azilian implements, though without the harpoon and Tardenoisean tools. It is important to note that though long-headed skulls predominate, a number of round-headed ones also occur and these show the further peculiarity that while the forehead is only moderately broad, the back of the skull is exceedingly wide. The occurrence of a round-headed people is of especial importance but their exact racial affinity is not yet clearly known. Another Tardenoisean burial containing round-headed skulls was found in the cave of Furfooz, in the valley of the Lesse, Belgium. This was discovered by Dupont in 1867. The industries associated with the burial rest on a Magdalenian layer; they are typical and reindeer bones occur. In Belgium, however, the tundra fauna continued to exist into early Mesolithic times being contemporary with the stag and forest fauna further south.

Another burial, apparently of Tardenoisean date, has been found near the mill called Axpea close to Tres Puntes, Alava(13), in the vicinity of Vittoria, Spain. In this case the burial is under a tumulus, which itself shows evidence for a certain amount of revêtment, and stones gathered in the vicinity have been heaped together. On excavation the following section was determined: on the top was a capping of vegetable earth intermixed with stones, below which occurred a layer of black earth a foot or two in thickness, under this was found another layer of clay full of stones, which rested directly on a natural limestone bottom. As there was a slight depression in the limestone at the spot chosen by Tardenoisean man, the total height of the tumulus above the general level of the ground was not more than about a yard. All the archaeological finds came from the black layer lying between the upper turfy layer and the underlying clay with boulders. No complete skulls but a number of human remains were found, as well as fragments of oxen. Lower jaws of at least five adult individuals and the fragment of the jaw of a child were observed. In these jaws there were still a number of teeth. Besides as many as 159 isolated teeth, some of them from upper jaws, were found. Flint tools, comprising knife blades and typical little geometric flints, as well as traces of ochre, were collected, also little pierced beads made from fragments of shell. In spite of the fact that one or two scraps of a sort of vague pottery, of very poor manufacture, were also observed, the industries point definitely to a latish Tardenoisean culture.

Another important site—of late Tardenoisean date, at earliest, as the trapeze occurs—is in the marshy valley of Mughem (14) near the Tagus. There are several tumuli, the most important being that called Cabeço d'Arruda. This consists of an oval tumulus 7 metres high built on ground rising some 5 metres above the level of the marshy land around; its longer diameter is about 100 metres, its shorter 60 metres. The contents of this hillock include shells, chipped flints, cinders and fragments of stone, as well as human skeletons. The shells, which are those of *Lutraria compressa*, *Tapes*, a small variety of *Cardium*, *Ostrea*, *Buccinum*, *Nucula*, *Pecten* and *Solen*, are only found to-day by the salt water far away. Clearly, then, when the folk lived at Mughem the sea was there, though to-day it is over twenty-five miles away and the land has risen considerably. The fauna includes stag, sheep, horse, pig, and dog, etc.; the industry, which is poor and rare, consists of small flakes, pigmies, the trapeze and rough bone awls. A small pebble pierced for suspension and possibly used as an ornament was also found. A little very poor pottery occurred, but only in the top layers of the mound. The industries, and the fauna alone, might suggest a Kitchen Midden Age and culture, but the considerable earth movement that has since taken place would argue for a slightly earlier, i.e. Tardenoisean, date.

As regards the famous "Grenelle" human remains, found in the alluvium near Paris in 1870, no accurate data as to the find exist, and it is not safe to base any theory on a find of human remains when the exact age is quite uncertain. Another burial under tumulus, where quantities of small pigmies occurred, but this time associated with cremation, has been described by L. Abbot as found near Sevenoaks.

ASTURIAN CULTURE(15)

The Asturian culture has only comparatively recently been recognised. It has been so named by its discoverer, Conde de la Vega del Sella, from the Province in North Spain where it was first noted, and where its occurrence is so plentiful. The remains of this culture consist apparently of kitchen middens or dust-bin rubbish thrown away into convenient caves, and is formed mainly of tests of shell-fish, which have been cemented together by stalagmitic growth into a compact deposit. A small industry has been determined including a new type of tool or pick made by roughly pointing a hard river pebble, but leaving its under-surface entirely untrimmed (see Plate 1, fig. 2). Smooth, round pebbles, probably used as rubbers or sometimes as hammer stones, also occur, as well as a few bone borers and two or three stag's tines pierced with a hole, differing from, though vaguely recalling, a simple form of Palaeolithic "bâton."

But in spite of the occurrence—literally in hundreds —of this new type of tool, the industry of the Asturian culture is not its most interesting feature. Many of the caves into which this rubbish was thrown already contained Palaeolithic deposits, and it has thus been possible to determine accurately the stratigraphical sequence. The Asturian industries are always resting on, and therefore younger than, layers containing typical Azilian tools; it is clear, therefore, that it was only in post-Azilian times that these masses of shells and rubbish were thrown into the caves or rock shelters, until they often became nearly filled up with the material. Subsequent denuding action has in many cases removed the greater part of this Asturian rubbish, but patches of midden material adhering to the ceilings and in crannies high up on the walls of the caves attest the fact that the original heaps were much greater in volume even than those that still exist; and when one considers the enormous mass of material still to be seen in such a cave as La Franca, it is necessary to postulate either a very large or very greedy population, which is not likely, or the lapse of a very considerable time during which these folk were living on shell-fish in North Spain.

FAUNA

As has been said these middens consist mainly of tests of shell-fish, but the following fauna[15] has been observed by the Count in the course of his investigations:

Equus caballus (horse)	*Bos* (ox)
Sus scrofa (pig)	*Cervus elaphus* (red deer)[1]
Capra pyrenaica (izard)[1]	*Cervus capreolus* (roe deer)
Capella rupicapra (chamois)[2]	*Mustela putoris* (pole-cat)
Lutra vulgaris (otter)	*Meles taxus* (badger)
Canis vulpes (wolf)	*Felis catus* (wild cat)
Lepus timidus (hare)	

The shell-fish are of the following species:

Patella, both medium and small size (very common)
Trochus lineatus (very common)
Cardium edule (very common)
Nassa reticulata (frequent)
Tuberculata atlantica (rare)
Mytilus edulis (rare)
Ostrea edulis (frequent)
Triton nodiferus (frequent)
Echinus (very common)
Cancer pagurus (frequent)
Portunus puber (very common)

Two species of land molluscs, viz.:

Helix nemoralis and *Helix arbustorum*

[1] Existed in historical times in North Spain.
[2] Exists to-day in the Picos de Europa.

A study of the fauna is important as giving us a clue to the climatic conditions and possibly to the period to which this culture should be assigned. It will be noticed that whereas on the one hand *Littorina* shells, common in Palaeolithic deposits, and on the other *Mytilus edulis*, common in deposits of true Neolithic or Copper Age, hardly occur, the typical shell of these Asturian rubbish heaps is the *Trochus*. This is very significant, for *Littorina litorea* is found to-day in the Atlantic and not in the Mediterranean, while the *Trochus* occurs in both. This latter shell is therefore a more warmth-loving mollusc than the *Littorina*. As to-day both occur in the sea off the north coast of Spain and the *Littorina* is not found in the middens, it follows that the climate of Asturian times was probably rather warmer than that of Asturias to-day. Again, the occurrence of a large number of *Helix nemoralis* shells in the upper layers of the midden would seem to indicate that damp conditions set in towards the end of this time. It has been claimed that the climate during the Kitchen Midden period in Denmark was also rather warmer than that of the same region to-day, an indication perhaps of the contemporaneity of the Asturian and Kitchen Midden cultures. The absence, however, of the Campignian axe and other tools typical of the kitchen middens of the Baltic area shows that we are not by any means dealing with one and the same culture, and this is further attested by the absence of pottery or of any kind of domestic animal in the Asturian remains.

The distribution of this culture has not yet been fully determined; it certainly occurs eastward of Asturias at Biarritz and as far away as Catalonia; possibly, also, there is a hint of it in the north of France.

MAGLEMOSEAN CULTURE

The focus of the Maglemosean culture is undoubtedly Denmark and the coasts of the Baltic. Although isolated finds have been discovered as far south as near Boulogne, as far east as Finland[1] and in south-east Yorkshire to the west, this culture was distinctly restricted in its distribution.

Danish prehistorians are apt to divide the prehistoric periods of their country into an Older and a Newer Stone Age. This is perhaps a little unfortunate, as, to the average student of Western Europe, the Old Stone Age refers to Palaeolithic times, and nothing definitely Palaeolithic has been demonstrated with certainty from the Baltic areas. Old Stone Age in Denmark refers not to the Palaeolithic but to Mesolithic industries and includes the Maglemosean and Shell Mound cultures, while the Danish New Stone Age comprises everything post-Shell Mound in date and earlier than the introduction of metal into the country. As this introduction took place very late in Scandinavia, the Danish New Stone Age includes cultures that we should class as true Neolithic, as well as others of rather later date, where, though the industries are still made of flint and stone, the culture has been influenced by and coincides in date with the Copper Age cultures of more favoured lands elsewhere in Europe, where ores of this metal had been early discovered.

Before considering the various Mesolithic industries of the Baltic area, a word or two must be said as to the geological conditions. During most of the Palaeolithic Period, except perhaps during the long warm Inter-

---

[1] Also certainly in Poland(19).

Glacial interlude corresponding to Penck's Mindel-Riss, Scandinavia, lying so far to the north and comprising high mountainous areas, was covered with immense ice sheets. During the last phase of glacial activity the southern border of this ice sheet ran roughly through the middle of Mecklenburg and the northern provinces of Germany, where the remains of its terminal moraine can still be traced. The presence of this immense ice sheet had profoundly affected the climate of the area generally; England, especially East Anglia, was long under its influence, and much of the difficulty in correlating English Quaternary chronology with that of areas further south must be attributed to the fact that the ice sheets of Scandinavia did not allow such small changes of temperature to manifest themselves as was the case further south; for, except perhaps during the Mindel-Riss Inter-Glaciation, East Anglia had little in the way of warm Inter-Glacial periods. The anti-cyclonic influence of a great ice mass as far south as Scandinavia must have been considerable. Again, the weight of such an ice mass has to be remembered; the earth's crust is by no means solid and even to-day Scandinavia is not a completely stable area. It is demonstrable that the peninsula is not unlike a gigantic seesaw, the south sinking, the north rising about a central stable line, and that this movement is as much as several inches a century. With the post-Glacial changes of climate the ice sheet began rapidly to retreat and the shores of the Baltic for the first time for many a century lay open for mankind to inhabit. Owing to the depression in the earth created by the ice mass, when the ice retreated from the Baltic area a great sea known as the Yoldia Sea was exposed, open to the north and to the west by wide channels connecting it with both the Arctic Ocean and with what is now the North Sea. But the removal of the ice pressure rapidly led, through isostatic movements, to an elevation of the area. The Baltic became a lake, completely cut off from both the Arctic Ocean and the North Sea; this lake is known as the Ancylus Lake from a small shell then abundant therein. It was at this period that pines were especially numerous, and it is to this time and just after it that the Maglemosean culture in question must be assigned. But just as a pendulum swings so far and then swings back, so the land underwent another depression which opened a wide channel from the Ancylus Lake to the North Sea, though it was not sufficient to reopen any connection with the Arctic Ocean. The new sea thus formed is named the Littorina Sea from the abundance of the shell *Littorina litorea* therein contained. By now the pine had, for the most part, been replaced by the oak and the Maglemosean culture by that of the Kitchen Middens. Thereafter a further slight elevation took place, but not sufficient to close the connection with the North Sea, a connection which, though much reduced, still exists to-day through the "Belts." The oak then gave place to the beech and the birch, and the Shell Mound or Kitchen Midden industries to those of the true Neolithic and later cultures.

The geologist, therefore, has enabled the prehistorian to obtain a fairly definite stratigraphical sequence for these early Baltic cultures. The presence of the pine, as well as of Ancylus fauna including the pine partridge, a bird never found far removed from pine forests, demonstrates conclusively the Ancylus Age for the Maglemosean culture, while the occurrence of the Shell Mound industry in association with the oak at a slightly later date shows us that this Kitchen Midden culture must be assigned to the Littorina period[1]. That the kitchen middens are later in date than the Maglemosean finds can be also proved on typological grounds, for some tool types which were abundant in Maglemosean times are also found in the lower layers of the shell mounds or kitchen middens, though not in the upper layers. They cannot therefore have had their origin in Shell Mound times and been passed on to a Maglemosean folk at a later date.

The earliest evidence for the presence of mankind in the Baltic area consists of three or four roughly made bone picks or, more properly speaking, hafts made of reindeer antler. Unfortunately the finds are isolated and there is no stratigraphy and but little detail is available as to the circumstances of their discovery. But as antler tools of Maglemosean and Kitchen Midden times are always made of stag's antler, it is reasonable to presume that these few examples were left by some earlier hunters who had drifted up from the south at a time when the country was hardly yet habitable. Following on this scanty evidence come the rich finds of Maglemosean date, and these in turn are replaced in certain areas by the culture of the Shell Mounds or Kitchen Middens. It would seem that the old Maglemosean culture continued to survive in certain parts of the hinterland of the Baltic area developing on its own even well into true Neolithic times, unaffected by contact with the more highly developed cultures of the coast. It is very probable that the so-called Arctic culture is nothing more nor less than the continued development of the old Maglemosean culture, with possible additions from the Shell Mound times.

[1] In some regions such as Finland the Maglemosean continued to exist right into the period of the oaks.

The Shell Mound folks under influences from the south-west developed the idea of the megalithic tombs, while the so-called "comb pottery" was introduced from the north-east. The true Neolithic industries then arose. These will be dealt with in the chapter on the Northern and Western Areas.

The type station of the Maglemosean Mesolithic culture is in the Maglemose or great bog of Mullerup, on the west of the island of Zealand (16).

Another site of very considerable importance has been discovered in the south of Zealand at Svaerdborg (17) where the section is as follows: At the base is found a thin layer of sand which is covered by shelly mud; on this shelly mud but under two distinct overlying peat layers rests the Maglemosean industry, its stratigraphical position being perfectly definite and clear. The two overlying peat layers are in their turn covered by the grass and humus of the modern heath land. These Zealand heaths are dry in summer but, especially in their lower areas, tend to become waterlogged in a wet winter, and correspond closely to some of the drier Irish bogs. They were evidently formerly lakes which have been filled in. Thus at Svaerdborg the bottom layers are of sand and shelly mud, and to-day the site is but little above sea level. The Maglemosean folk seem to have lived on the banks of these lakes, or even on rafts of some sort in the shallow water at the margin.

The Maglemosean industries, in the various sites

---

[1] It is obvious the name Maglemosean or "Great Bogian" given to this culture is far from sensible. If a type station name must be given to the culture, it would be much more reasonable to call it Mullerupian. Still as the name Maglemose has come definitely into the literature of the subject and prehistorians have learnt to understand what is meant by it, it would be difficult or well-nigh impossible to introduce any new term.

which have been excavated, are not absolutely uniform. For example, Svaerdborg has yielded innumerable small pigmy tools, whereas only a few examples of them have come from the type station of Mullerup itself. When describing the industry, therefore, it must be remembered that the results of the diggings in various sites are here combined.

The tools fall readily into two groups: first, those made from flint, and secondly, those made from bone or antler. The material used for the latter was generally obtained from the stag, although elk and roe buck, etc., were sometimes used. Shed antlers were usually utilised.

FLINT TOOLS (Plate 4)

Flint tools include pigmies, scrapers (both core and on flakes), picks, a small number—not at all typical—of a tool known as the Campigny axe which is found abundantly in the kitchen middens and will there be described.

The pigmies recall those of the Tardenoisean culture but, as has been said, this is not surprising in view of the fact that for a composite tool only certain shapes are really convenient; they include triangles, generally rather elongated and of scalene form, one short and one long edge being carefully blunted, the other long edge being left sharp. The uses and methods of hafting these little tools will be discussed later. We also have to note little blunted backs, lunates and blunt-ended flakes with little notched shoulders. One beautifully made, finely pointed shoulder point from Holmegaards Mose may be noted. Nothing particular need be said as to the scrapers. They are of the usual kind and range from a rough core and a sort of keel-scraper to fine scrapers on the end of blades. Round oval scrapers are also found.

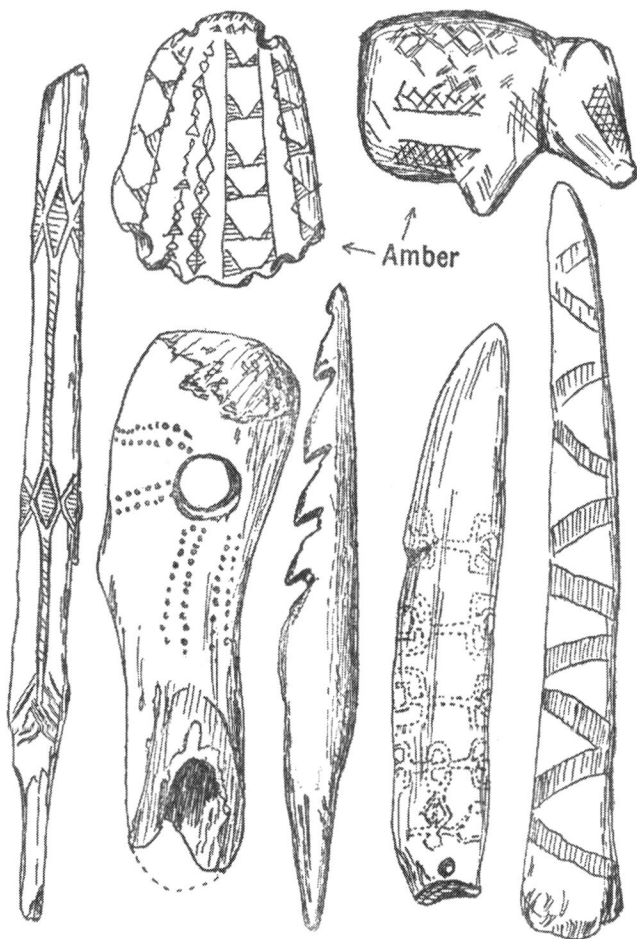

Plate 3 (for legend and description, see p. 34).

LEGEND AND EXPLANATION OF PLATES 3 AND 4

Plate 3 shows examples of Maglemosean bone tools, often decorated. A typical harpoon is figured as well as an antler adze or haft—that an adze not an axe was desired is clear from the direction of the round hafting hole. Most of the decoration is purely geometric, but that on the bone spatula to the right of the harpoon probably represents conventionalised human beings. The two amber figurines alas have no provenance, but very possibly belong to this Maglemose culture.

Plate 4 shows examples from Svaerdborg. Note, on the left, the pigmy tools so common at this site, the core below, and alongside it a small round scraper; on the right the pick, and below it a small edition hafted as an adze. The bone tools are important. There is a hafted antler point, a pierced tooth ornament and a bone point armed along its sides with small sharp flakes hafted in longitudinal grooves. Such tools with the flints still in place, attached by a mastic possibly made from amber, have been found.

The hafting of these pigmy tools—as well as those of the Tardenoisean culture—is of interest, and below are two drawings to illustrate how it was probably done. Naturally the matter is largely conjectural.

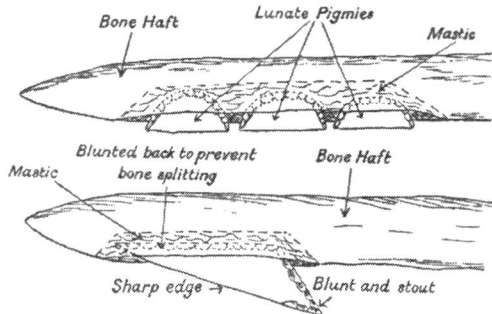

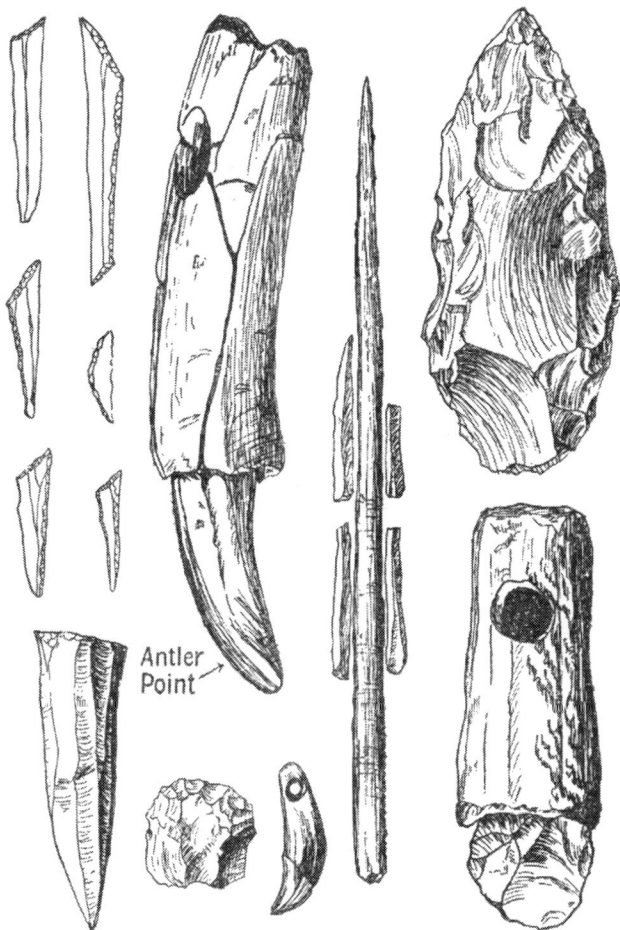

Antler
Point →

Plate 4 (for legend and description, see p. 34).

The picks resemble the Kitchen Midden or Campigny picks, though as a rule they are considerably smaller in size. There is nothing particular to mention in regard to the simple cores and flakes.

ANTLER AND BONE TOOLS (Plate 3)

The most typical tool of the culture, a small, narrow harpoon barbed on one side, is contained in this series. The barbs vary in number from one near the point to many along one side of the shaft. It is the "type fossil" of the Maglemosean industries, and does not survive even in a modified form into Shell Mound or Kitchen Midden times, except perhaps in one single instance at Havelse Ros, Kildefjord, where a few harpoons have been unearthed apparently of very early Kitchen Midden Age, though with their enormous coarse barbs they have very little likeness to the slender, beautifully worked true Maglemosean harpoon. Bone points, occasionally eyed when they become needles, have been discovered, as well as various forms of fish hook. The bone points themselves were doubtless used as awls and are often of considerable size. They were easily made, a suitable bit of bone or antler being merely rounded and pointed, no attempt being made to form anything like a regular needle. The fish hooks are sometimes V-shaped; sometimes one limb is longer than another, thus (✓). One of the most interesting bone tools consists of a bone point grooved along its length, sometimes only on one side of the stem, sometimes on both; in these grooves attached by some suitable mastic, possibly manufactured from amber, were laid little flint flakes or pigmy tools; specimens have been actually found with the flints still in position. They must have made very efficient lance points or darts, the end of the bone forming the point and the row of sharp flint flakes giving either a single or double edge to the weapon. These very delightful tools survive in the base of the shell mounds, as is proved by their being found at Kasemose. Bone chisels are of common occurrence and there is little of importance to remark about them. They are made on a long bone, the end of which has been carefully rounded and sharpened. In some cases they approximate rather to the polishers or spatulae of Palaeolithic times than to actual chisels.

The most numerous and perhaps the most character-istic objects in the Maglemosean industries are the pierced antler tools and hafts. In general a portion of antler is chosen, usually about two inches in diameter and seven or eight inches in length; it is selected from near the thickened base of an antler, thereby ensuring considerable strength even when the hole is pierced for hafting purposes. It is very rare for a piece of antler to be prepared by being cut off at both ends, and so with-out a natural thickened base, though this method, on the other hand, is in common use in the Shell Mound period of a later date. At this point we must differentiate two uses: in the first the portion of the antler is itself the tool, in the second it is only the haft in which a small stone is inserted as the working edge. In both cases, however, the antler in question was itself hafted, pos-sibly on a wooden staff, as is proved by its being pierced by a more or less rounded hole. It is important to note the direction of this hole relative to the working edge either of the antler, when it is itself the tool, or of the stone hafted into an oval hole scooped out at the end of the antler. Where the direction of the hole is parallel to the working edge, the tool, when hafted, is an axe. Where, on the other hand, the direction of the hole is at right angles to the working edge, the tool is an adze. This will be clearly seen on reference to Plates 3 and 4. It is interesting to note that in Maglemosean times the adze is a far commoner tool than the axe, while later, in Shell Mound times, the axe is more frequently found.

Animals' teeth pierced for ornament are not unknown, and the Maglemosean hunter was not averse to a certain amount of decoration. His bone tools are often ornamented with a series of fine engraved lines and punctuations forming geometric patterns, such as zigzags, lozenges and the like. More or less naturalistic figures of animals have been found in Jutland, and in at least one instance it is interesting to recognise conventionalisation of the human form as a decorative motif (Plate 3). Several rough little sculptures of animals carved in amber have also been collected, and, though there is no absolute certainty as to their date, Danish prehistorians are inclined to class them as Maglemosean[18]. It must always be remembered that accurate dating is by no means easy; the Maglemosean industries are found near the surface, and we are not dealing with a simple state of affairs, such as a Palaeolithic cave deposit completely sealed in by stalagmite!

The general distribution of this culture has already been given, attested by the discovery of the typical harpoon in the various regions. As regards south-east Yorkshire, not only were two typical harpoons found, but also a small stone industry, and it is possible that some of the apparently early pigmy tools found on the surface of East Anglia generally will have in the end to be assigned to this culture.

The origin of the Maglemosean folk remains to a certain extent a mystery. If we except the one or two finds of reindeer bone, already mentioned, that seem to have been left by chance by some still earlier hunter, Maglemosean man was the first inhabitant of Denmark, southern Scandinavia, and the Baltic area generally. Like the Tardenoisean he was aware of the advantages of a composite tool, but there is no reason for inter-relating the two cultures. The occurrence of a certain amount of art might suggest Upper Palaeolithic con-nections, but, except in one or two instances found in Jutland, the absence of well-drawn naturalistic figures would militate against there having been any connection with the Magdalenians of France. On the other hand, if we turn to the Upper Palaeolithic of Moravia, a region where Magdalenian man does not seem to have penetrated though his influence was undoubtedly felt, we find an Aurignacian culture developing on its own lines, contemporary in part with the French Magdalenian culture but exhibiting a different art which has perhaps slightly greater affinity to the Maglemosean. Should future investigations demonstrate that this is the case we should have to consider the Maglemosean culture as being a child of the Upper Palaeolithic culture of eastern and central Europe, driven north-west into the still inhospitable, but now ice-free, area of the Baltic by the pressure of the on-coming true Neolithic folk who were themselves slowly advancing from Central Asia probably forced thence by the ever-increasing drought of regions that had previously been so suitable for human development. It may be noted that industries similar to the Maglemosean have been recognised in Poland[19].

No burials of Maglemosean date have been noted, but lately some skeletal remains have been found in the peat, including a lower jaw, said to show Palaeolithic affinities.

KITCHEN MIDDENS(20)

Under the old classification Kitchen Middens or Shell Mounds are described as belonging to the Neolithic Period because a certain amount of pottery is found in them, and, although other domestic animals are for the most part absent, the dog is common. However, actually in the field, it is not easy to distinguish between the Maglemosean and the Kitchen Midden industries, and the close affinity that exists between the two cultures cannot be too strongly urged.

The shell mounds or kitchen middens consist, as their name implies, of masses of shell-fish and other kitchen refuse that has been cast aside by man; they are glorified dust bins. These masses have become cemented together and form to-day veritable hillocks, often covering immense areas. They have been known to measure as much as 100 yards in length by 50 in breadth by 1 yard high. The quantity of shell-fish consumed by these primitive folk, who seem to have largely subsisted on this diet, is prodigious. The industries (Plate 5) obtained from the shell mounds include, as in the case of the Maglemosean culture, both stone and bone tools, but in this case we also have a poorly formed pottery made of an inferior coarse paste. The pots are commonly cylindrical, with rounded, or sometimes pointed, bases, and expand slightly at the top to form a rim. The stone industry includes the typical transverse-edge arrow head and the Campigny axe (Plate 5, *b* or Plate 11, no. 12 and Plate 5, *c*). The latter is formed on a piece of flint or split stone pebble by squaring the sides, removing a large flake at one end and so obtaining a cutting edge by the intersection of this flake with the flat under-surface of the piece of flint or split pebble. As has been

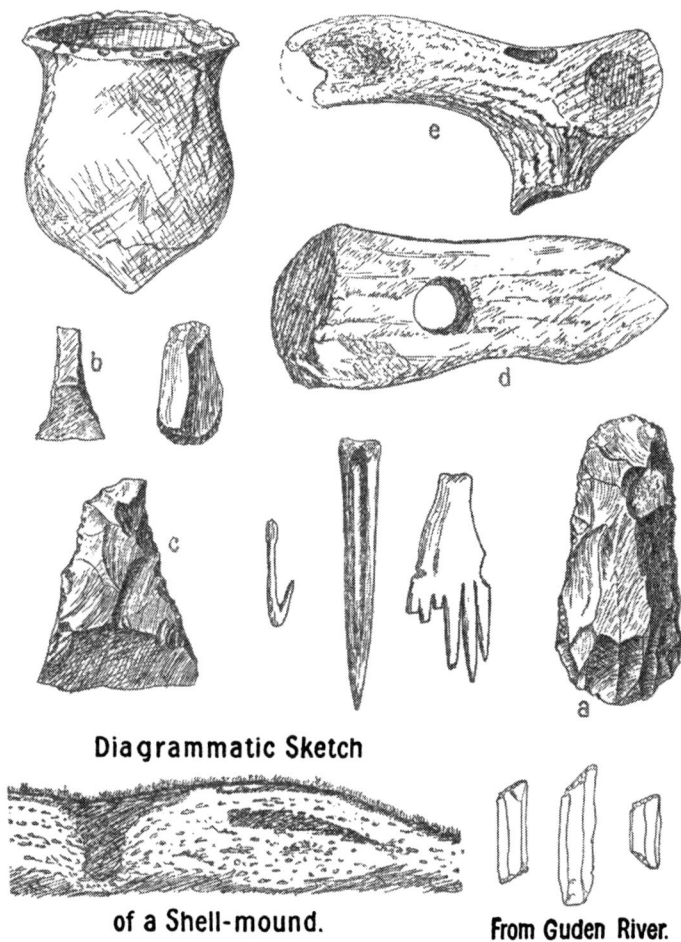

Diagrammatic Sketch

of a Shell-mound.

From Guden River.

Plate 5. Examples of pottery and tools from the kitchen middens and shell mounds.

noted, only two or three examples at most, and these only approximating to this type, have been found among the Maglemosean industries, but they are very common in the shell mounds. As always, scrapers, both core and on flakes, are common, and some very fine examples made on the ends of blades have been discovered. Neolithic picks are also common (Plate 5, *a*) and range from comparatively large examples down to small fine tools, so beautifully chipped that at first sight they almost recall Proto-Solutrean laurel leaves. Awls, often of the Campigny type with irregular trimming up the point, may be noted, sometimes small in size, sometimes comparatively coarse and large. Small fine examples are sometimes made at the concave or bevelled end of a blade, thus forming as it were the two horns of a scooped-out crescent, sometimes the awls are long and medial, somewhat resembling the base end of a "Font Robert" point if broken in half. Cores, both small and of immense size—recalling those found at various sites near Liège, Belgium—and flakes occur in any quantity, as well as hammer stones and rough chopping tools. So-called "fabricators" are not infrequent, as well as little transverse-edge arrow points with carefully squared blunted sides, and the trapeze pigmy tool. Polished or ground tools have not been found, except occasionally at the extreme top of shell mounds (and therefore at the very end of the period) where a few examples have been observed doubtless heralding the beginning of the true New Stone Age of Denmark.

The bone or antler industry, made, as in Maglemosean times, mainly from stag's antler, includes awls and chisels, and especially the type, already described under the Maglemosean antler industry, where a portion of antler is taken, pierced for hafting, and one end prepared either for use itself as a working edge or for the hafting of a stone tool. In the shell mounds it is the axe rather than the adze that seems to have been commonly required, as is attested by the direction of the hafting hole through the portion of antler relative to the working edge of the tool. Although, as before, Shell Mound man usually prepared a portion of antler at the base of a tine where it thickens, so as to ensure strength for the hole pierced for hafting, yet we now often find that he deemed it sufficient merely to cut off a portion of antler at both ends and to use this for his purpose (compare on Plate 5, *d* and *e*). Front teeth of animals carefully ground and prepared to form gouges may be noted, and the very rare survivals into Shell Mound times of a coarse form of Maglemosean harpoon, as well as of the bone points fitted with flakes along their sides, has already been noted. The use of wood for hafting purposes is not only inferred but proved by the actual finding of examples with the stone tools still attached to their wooden hafts. Coming to objects of decoration, etc., we note something of the nature of small combs from at least one site, as well as a few pendants. Ornamentation in the form of a lozenge pattern in fine engraved lines has been observed on an antler haft, but art as a whole is far less common in Shell Mound than in Maglemosean times. We are dealing with a rich, if primitive, culture, though mainly that of the hunter. In spite of the presence of pottery the sickle has not been found, therefore agriculture, if practised at all, was extremely rare. Again, domestic animals are represented almost entirely by the dog, and polished tools are absent. Perhaps the nearest analogous culture was that of the Strandloopers of South Africa, who, like these northern folk, lived mainly near the coast and subsisted almost entirely on shell-fish.

Burials in the kitchen middens are not unknown.

The body is often found simply laid out full length, though sometimes it is outlined, as it were, by a few big stones placed round it at intervals. Nothing in the nature of careful ceremonial burial has been observed.

A comparison of the Maglemosean and Shell Mound cultures would not be out of place at this point. It should be observed in passing that whereas shell mounds are common in Jutland and rare in Zealand, exactly the opposite is the case for the Maglemosean industries. Again, it would appear that Shell Mound folk lived exclusively by the coasts, whereas this was not necessarily the case with regard to their Maglemosean forerunners. It is true that shell mounds are often found to-day far from the sea shore, but this can be explained by the fact that the level of the land has changed so that mounds that once were close to the sea are now far inland; in flat areas like Denmark very small changes in the relative levels of land and sea will cause very great differences in the position of sites. Perhaps some of the connections and differences between the two cultures can be best expressed in condensed form.

The bone points studded longitudinally with flakes that flourish in the Maglemosean times only just survive into the base of the shell mounds. On the other hand, the transverse-edge arrow heads with small square blunted sides appear very rarely, or not at all, in the earlier industry, but flourish in Shell Mound industries and even survive into true Neolithic times. Again, the adze is common in the Maglemosean tools and the axe considerably rarer, whereas in Shell Mound times the exact opposite is the case, the axe being by far the more usual tool. Antler hafts, cut off at both ends, as already described, are extremely rare in Maglemosean sites, though this was a common mode of preparing the tool among the Shell Mound folk. Then the typical Maglemosean harpoon disappears with this culture and, practically speaking, no harpoon of this kind is found in the kitchen middens. Finally the trapeze form of pigmy tool only appears with the coming of the Shell Mound culture, though it survives well into true Neolithic times.

Enough has been said to show that these two cultures are distinct, although there is a close affinity between them, and for anyone who has studied the two on the spot it is impossible to separate them as belonging to two totally different civilisations.

An industry, said to be of intermediate type and date, has lately been recognised near Gothenburg in south-western Sweden, and certain pigmy finds—though including trapezes—from by the Guden River in Jutland also seem to belong to a very late Maglemosean stage of culture in course of transition to Shell Mound types.

The extent of the Kitchen Midden culture is not easy to determine with certainty, as, though different, there seems to be close connection between it and the Campignian of Western Europe, which it will be our next business briefly to describe. The origin of the Shell Mound culture is also unknown, although one might perhaps hazard a guess that the Maglemosean on the one hand and the Campignian on the other both had a share in its formation.

An allied culture, doubtless derived from the same stock as that of the shell mounds, occurs in Norway. It survived late, there being admixture with polished celts. Rock rather than flint is preferred for toolmaking. The name Nöstvet—a site near Oslo—has been suggested for this culture.

CAMPIGNIAN CULTURE

The Campignian is another of these Mesolithic cultures that, under the old classification, was classed as early Neolithic owing to the presence of coarse pottery and a few rare examples of domesticated animals [1].

The type stations of Campigny are to be found near the little town of Blangy-sur-Bresle, not far from Bouillancourt-en-Séry in the Department of the Seine-Inférieure (21). The site consists of a number of land habitations in the form of *fonds de cabanes* [2]. The pits are oval in shape and vary in size, being sometimes as much as 5 yards in the longer diameter. The following section is vouched for by M. Capitan. At the base a clayey chalk, above which occur gravels containing mammoth bones. The huts are hollowed in this gravel and at the bottom of them were found the cinders and charcoal of a Campignian hearth. Above these cinders was a yellow sandy loam infilling, containing Campignian tools. On the top was modern humus containing, it is stated, a few polished stone tools. Should the section really be as here given, it will be noted that the Campignian is stratigraphically post-Quaternary and earlier than the true Neolithic, as attested by the presence of polished stone tools in the overlying humus. The industries themselves comprise the Campignian axe already described, as well as the pick and transverse-edge arrow head. There are

[1] A number of prehistorians are rather inclined to-day to claim that the original excavation at Campigny was not well done and that no proofs for the existence of a separate early culture at this spot can be made out. This is largely due to the late M. de Morgan, who claimed to have found a polished celt in a hearth—doubtless derived from the overlying Neolithic humus! The tools collected at Campigny and the similar industries found in Belgium, France and elsewhere resemble those found in the shell mounds, and it is hardly wise to summarily deny the existence of this Mesolithic culture. All Campigny industries, however, are not of the same age, survivals occur showing admixture with more recent objects.

[2] For description of *fonds de cabanes* see chapter III.

also rough awls, scrapers, flakes, cores, etc. The rare finds of one or two burin-like tools probably indicate a reminiscence of older Palaeolithic times. The fauna at Campigny consisted only of fragments and species are difficult to determine, but the ox, the horse, and the stag have been recognised. The charcoal was examined and included identifiable remains of oak and ash, as well as remains of other trees that could not be determined. Taking the Cámpignian axe (Plate 5, c) as the type tool, with perhaps also the large rough awl and the roughly made pick, the absence of any polished industry or well made pottery being also a characteristic, the existence of this Campignian Mesolithic culture can be demonstrated over large areas of north-western Europe. The culture was common in Belgium, probably also in our own country, as well as in the north of France. Further south in the Mediterranean basin the Campignian is not so common, because that district is nearer the focus of the older Tardenoisean culture, which culture seems to have persisted with little change, except for the introduction of the trapeze and the disappearance of the burin, until true Neolithic times.

Mesolithic times as a whole are perhaps rather unprogressive and present scenes of primitive culture little relieved by either wealth of industries or beauty of art. But with the arrival of the Neolithic civilisation among these primitive people a sudden change took place and cultures containing the germs of many modern developments soon grew up and progressed rapidly.

BIBLIOGRAPHY AND REFERENCES

(1) E. PIETTE. Many articles in *L'Anthropologie* round about 1895 deal with his various Pyrenaean excavations. But one of the best sections at Mas d'Azil that he describes appeared in 1892, *Assoc. fr. pour l'av. des Sc., Congrès de Pau.*

(2) R. MUNRO. For an excellent brief account of the Scottish Mesolithic sites, see *Prehistoric Britain* (Home University Series).
A. H. BISHOP. "An Oronsay shell-mound...." *Proc. Soc. of Antiq. of Scotland*, vol. XLVIII.

(3) M. C. BURKITT. An illustration of these paintings can be seen in the Presidential Address to the Prehistoric Society of East Anglia for 1925. Vol. V, pt 1.

(4) M. H. MÜLLER. "Une station paléolithique en plein Vercors, Tunnel de Bobache (Drôme)." *Assoc. fr. pour l'av. des Sc., Congrès de Reims*, 1907.
—— "Nouvelles fouilles à la station paléolithique de Bobache (Vercors)." *Soc. d'Anth. de Lyon*, 5 Nov. 1910.

(5) F. SARASIN. "Die steinzeitlichen stationen des Birstales zwischen Basel und Delsberg." *Nouveaux Mémoires de la Société Helvétique des Sciences Naturelles.* Vol. LIV, 1918.

(6) E. RAHIR. *L'Habitat tardenoisien des Grottes de Remouchamps.* 1921.

(7) H. BREUIL and H. OBERMAIER. "Les premiers travaux de l'Institut de Paléontologie humaine." *L'Anthropologie*, tome XXIII, 1912.

(8) G. PATIRI. *L'Arte Minuscula paleolitica dell' officina Termitana nella grotta del Castello in Termini-Imerese.* 1910.

(9) L. LEQUEUX. For the best account of the Belgian Mesolithic industries see: "Stations tardenoisiennes des vallées de l'Amblève, de la Vesdre et de l'Ourthe," Communication made to the Soc. d'Anth. de Bruxelles, 4 March 1923; "Emplacements d'habitations tardenoisiennes et objets néolithiques découverts à Langerloo," *ibid.*, 26 March 1923; "Industrie tardenoisienne à Cailloux roulés de Vossem (Brabant)," *ibid.*, 28 May 1923. The prehistoric site at Zonhoven is described in a short work by M. de Puydt and others called *Mélanges d'Archéologie préhistorique* and published at Liège.

(10) F. BUCKLEY. *A Microlithic Industry.* Privately printed (1921), Spottiswoode Ltd., Marsden, Yorks.

F. Buckley. "Yorkshire Graves." *Proc. Prehist. Soc. of E. Anglia*, vol. iii, pt 4, 1922.

—— *A Microlithic Industry of the Pennine Chain*. Privately printed. 1924.

(11) E. Cartailhac. *Les Grottes de Grimaldi*. Tome ii, fasc. 2. 1912.

(12) R. R. Schmidt. "Die Vorgeschichtlichen Kulturen der Ofnet." *Ber. d. Nat.-Wiss. Ver. f. Schwaben u. Neuberg*, 1908, pp. 87–107. For the question of decapitation see Comte Begouen's article in the *Bull. Soc. Prēhist. Française*, 29 March, 1912.

(13) P. R. de Azúa. "Sepultura tardenoisiense de Axpea." *Bol. de la Soc. española de hist. nat.*, Dec. 1918.

(14) E. Cartailhac. Still the best account is probably *Les Âges préhistoriques de l'Espagne et du Portugal*, p. 51. 1886.

(15) Vega del Sella. "El Asturiense." *Mem. Num. 32 of Com. de invest. pal. y prehist.* 1923.

(16) G. Sarauw. "En stenalders boplads i Maglemose ved Mullerup, sammenholdt med beslægtede fund." *Aarbøger for Nordisk Oldkyndighed og Historie*, 1903, ii række, 18 bind.

(17) K. F. Johansen. *"Une station du plus ancien âge de la pierre dans la tourbière de Svaerdborg." *Mém. de la Soc. Roy. des Antiq. du Nord*, 1918–19, published in 1920.

(18) S. Müller. For Prehistoric decorative art in Denmark *Oldtidens Kunst i Danmark* should be consulted—published in 1918.

(19) L. Kozlowski. See "L'époque Mésolithique en Pologne." *L'Anthropologie*, tome xxxvi, 1926.

(20) S. Müller and others. For a full description of the kitchen middens see *Affaldsdynger fra stenalderen i Danmark*, published in 1900 for the Nat. Museum at Copenhagen.

(21) L. Capitan. "Le Campignien." *Rev. de l'École d' Anth. de Paris*, 1898.

(22) C. de Mérejkowsky. "Recherches préliminaires sur l'âge de la pierre en Crimée." *Bull. Soc. russe de géographie*, tome xvi, 1880.

CHAPTER II

NEOLITHIC CIVILISATION

IT is by no means incorrect to employ the term *Neolithic Civilisation*. The difference between the life and conditions of the New Stone Age folk and those of their Palaeolithic forerunners is profound and not in any way to be compared with the smaller differences that exist for example between the various Mesolithic cultures. It will be our first duty, then, to consider what were the causes that led to this profound change in human life, and, as far as possible, how these various causes operated.

The most notable additions to human experience that we discover in Neolithic times are: (1) the practice of agriculture; (2) the domestication of animals; (3) the manufacture of pottery; (4) the grinding and polishing of stone tools, instead of, as formerly, shaping them merely by chipping.

It will of course be noted that the use of metal was still unknown among the true Neolithic folk of Western Europe but, for all that, knowledge of its possibilities was not far off, especially in areas like the Spanish Peninsula where copper ores occur in abundance, and it is highly probable that in the eastern Mediterranean metal was in use from very early times indeed, in fact during most of the period of the Neolithic or New Stone Age in western Europe.

AGRICULTURE AND THE DOMESTICATION OF ANIMALS

The influence of agriculture and of domestic animals on mankind's outlook on life is fundamental. Instead of small groups of men gaining a precarious livelihood by hunting, we find more or less settled communities growing up. To a hunting people the fear is ever present lest the game should fail to return at its usual time, and lest owing to their inability to store food-stuff for more than a short time, starvation may overcome them; but now we find villages with full granaries able to withstand difficult seasons. Naturally the difference must not be forced too far. Crops, like any other gift of nature, may suffer so severely through successive droughts and other natural disasters that, as in the case of the hunters, starvation may overtake the settled community; but there is much more chance of surviving such disasters, and of having a store sufficient to tide over difficult times, in the case of an agricultural people having flocks and herds, than in the case of mere hunters.

Agriculture and the domestication of animals not only engender community life and a relatively safer existence, but also introduce other changes into man's social habits. The change from the life of a small, sparse, hunting population to that of thickly populated villages introduces the necessity for a well-regulated community life. Actions that have little effect on isolated families may become seriously inconvenient in the comparatively crowded conditions of the village. Again the congregation into communities favours the growth of specialisation. In Palaeolithic times the man who had a special talent for chipping flint probably found himself promoted to be tool-maker for the party, and doubtless had his food hunted for him in return; but community life not only gives a tremendous impulse to such division of labour, but the introduction of the new arts of agriculture and stock-keeping not to speak of the new industry of village-building and repair gives scope for further specialisation. Again, the possession of crops and herds, whether owned by the individual, by the family, or by the community, involves the necessity for protection which was far less pressing in Palaeolithic times. The conception of property, now introduced for the first time in human history on anything like a large scale, involves automatically the conception of war. This war may have been, and doubtless largely was, a war against wild animals, who would be always prepared to prey upon the fat cattle or crops. To even the village idiot could be assigned the definite work of protecting the crops from the havoc of birds, as has been done in rural districts to our own times. But protection was also required against man himself who was presumably equally ready then, as now, to take somebody else's goods for himself if he could get hold of them. A bad season or two, supplies running low in a given community, what more natural than that they should attempt to plunder the folk near by in a more favoured district or possessing larger reserves.

Thus we find the introduction of agriculture and domestic animals, by necessitating community life, postulates not only specialisation, which is good for progress, but also the destructive element of aggression, and its corollary—defence. But, above all, the harnessing of nature and the consequent possession of reserves of food automatically brings into play the Malthusian Law, and as a result we note a rapid rise in population; this, in turn, has its natural repercussion both on specialisation and aggression. In a word the old order of things is coming to an end in western Europe and the modern world is being born with all its problems.

HUSBANDRY

We are still somewhat ignorant as to the various crops raised by Neolithic man and his methods of husbandry. Fortunately, however, certain Neolithic villages were built over the margins of shallow lakes for purposes of better protection, and a certain amount of material has been collected from the peat and mud below(1). Investigations have shown that in Switzerland the small-grained six-rowed barley (*Hordeum hexastichum sanctum*) and the small lake-dwelling wheat (*Triticum vulgare antiquorum*) were amongst the earliest and the most important of the various farinaceous crops cultivated. After these come the beardless compact wheat (*Triticum vulgare compactum muticum*) and the larger six-rowed barley (*Hordeum hexastichum densum*) and occasionally its two-rowed relative. With these latter occur two kinds of millet, the common millet (*Panicum miliaceum*) and the Italian millet (*Setaria italica*). The one-rowed wheat (*Triticum monococcum*), the two-rowed wheat (*Triticum dicoccum*), and the Egyptian wheat (*Triticum turgidum*) have also been found, but were by no means general. The oat and the spelt did not appear till a much later time—well into the Metal Ages—and rye has not been found. Of course it is not safe to assume that these crops were sown by Neolithic man all over Europe. As has been said, our knowledge is mainly derived from lake dwellings, more especially those of Switzerland, and these, as will be seen in the sequel, have but a limited distribution in area and belong to only one of the several branches into which Neolithic man can be divided. But in the few Neolithic sites, outside the Lake Dwelling areas, where farinaceous seeds have been collected and permit of study, the results indicate a similar state of affairs. Thus at Lengyel (Late Neolithic), in Hungary, the six-rowed barley has been noted, as well as the beardless wheat and the one-rowed wheat. Beardless wheat is also found at Butmir (Late Neolithic), a site near Serajevo, Bosnia (2).

Apples and pears, split and dried, have been observed, also the poppy (*Papaver somniferum*) and, although these were no doubt largely collected wild, the size of the former, at any rate, sometimes suggests a certain amount of care taken in their cultivation. The parsnip, carrot, pig weed, walnut and grape were certainly used, though these again may have been collected wild. Other berries, such as the raspberry, blackberry, etc., occurred abundantly wild, and there would be no need for their cultivation.

Although the staple clothing of Neolithic man was still made from the skins of wild and domestic animals, the peat under the old lake dwellings has preserved for us a certain amount of woven and plaited material indicating the knowledge and use of flax (*Linum angustifolium*); not only for the making of clothes, but also for other purposes, such as fishing nets, etc.

Three new implements would be necessary for the agriculturist: the first is a ploughing tool to prepare the ground; the second is a sickle to harvest the crops; the third a mortar or milling stone to reduce the grain to flour. The first of these may have taken the form of a ground or polished celt mounted adze-wise and used simply as a hoe, but it is quite likely there was also in use a wooden plough similar to the primitive pattern that is still sometimes seen to-day in out-of-the-way parts of such countries as Spain [1]. The obvious advantage of

[1] Rock carvings depicting ploughs drawn by oxen and directed by men have been found and belong to the Copper or Bronze Ages

some harder material for making the share must have been early realised, and it has been suggested, probably with truth, that some of the coarsely chipped, roughly pointed bars of flint or quartzite, such as have been found at a Neolithic site in the Forest of Montmorency, North France, were used for this purpose. Some of these bars are seven to nine inches long by about an inch and a half broad, and the idea is that they projected slightly from the end of a short wooden share to which they were attached. Although most of the strain would, of course, be borne by the wooden share, the quartzite bar would to some extent protect it.

Sickles are quite commonly found in Neolithic stations. They consist of a series of slightly curved, generally toothed, blades that were hafted lengthways in a sickle-shaped wooden handle (Plate 12, no. 5). Even when not toothed they can be identified with certainty by carefully examining the working edge and noting how continuous contact with the straw has produced a peculiar and characteristic polish and shine on the edge of the flint. The only other phenomenon in the least comparable to this appearance is the sand polish produced on flints by desert action. These wooden sickles, armed with their flint blades, continued in use even after the general introduction of metal, and they have been collected, complete with haft, from Egypt. What may well be such a wooden haft, judging from its size, can be seen painted on the walls of the rock shelter at Los Letreros near Velez Blanco, not far from Lorca

(Plate 28, fig. 1). Whether or not these ploughs were solely made of wood cannot be determined, but an Egyptian example stamped with the cartouch of Amenophis IV complete with share and coulter—the former made of hard wood—has lately been found in the tomb of Ramose, vizier to the Pharaoh.

in south-east Spain (Plate 30, fourth row). The art in this rock shelter is of Copper Age[1]. It is unlikely that these sickles would have been represented so large if they had been made of metal and no longer consisted of the old wooden haft with flints. For a long time after metal was introduced it was a very valuable commodity, and the sickles that are found even in Early Bronze Age times are comparatively small articles.

The mill consisted of (1) a slab of some hard rock or sandstone hollowed out to a greater or less extent with use, the surface being smooth, and (2) a sort of stone rolling pin with which the actual grinding process was performed.

In these early times probably nothing was realised as to the exhaustion of land, and so on, but with all the country around to choose from it would only be necessary to break up new ground and leave the old fields fallow for a period, a practice the advisability of which would be soon learnt by experience, even if the reason were not understood.

STOCK-RAISING

Considerable controversy has raged as to how far, if at all, Palaeolithic man had any notion of the domestication of animals. It is admitted that already in Azilian times the dog had come to live with man, for remains have been found at La Tourasse and Oban(3), and in the kitchen middens of Denmark bones of this animal have also been found. It is argued by many that certain engravings on bones of Magdalenian Age from Mas d'Azil show that horses had already been pressed into the service of man, as some lines on the heads of the animals definitely demonstrate the use of a halter. The

[1] For description of this group see chapter x.

opponents of this theory argue that the lines in question merely denote the muscles of the face and that there is no proof whatever that they were intended to represent harness.

At this point it may be well to define what is meant by the domestication of animals. Domestication is not the same thing as taming. The young of many wild animals (especially is this the case with foals) are not particularly timid in the presence of small encampments of men, and it is more than conceivable that after the Palaeolithic hunter had killed a dam for food the foal might be induced to take up his quarters and become tamed by his human neighbours. Once tamed there is no reason to refuse the possibility that he was made to do a little work in the way of drawing loads and so on, and for this purpose some form of simple harness made from reindeer thong would naturally be necessary. But for true domestication there must be the added factor of continuous breeding in captivity, and of this there is no evidence in Palaeolithic times. Nothing in the nature of a stable has yet been discovered in connection with the "homes," and the bones of the animals found in the deposits, as far as has yet been observed, are those of the wild species. Long domestication tends to produce new varieties and a certain thinning and fining in the bones, and this has not yet been observed in Palaeolithic sites.

It is admitted by most students of the subject that domestication first took place somewhere in the east, outside Europe, and the suggestion is made that this discovery had a close connection with the climatic changes which, as we shall see later in this chapter, were taking place in Central Asia, where the desert conditions that we find to-day were setting in. There is no better situation for the first domestication of animals than the oasis. An occasional tame individual would not give rise to the idea of breeding the species in captivity for the use of man, but a number of individuals forced by natural conditions to live near man, and there breeding normally, might start the notion, which would then be easily elaborated. An oasis in a country which was rapidly becoming more and more desert provides just this natural propulsion. Animals are forced to approach nearer and nearer to man, who can then with very little effort tame them and turn them to his uses, and the natural breeding that results would be noted and very soon regulated. When we turn to actual sites in Central Asia, such as Anau in Russian Turkestan(4), we find that the facts uphold this *a priori* reasoning. The deposits at Anau date back to very early days indeed, possibly corresponding in time to the Upper Palaeolithic of western Europe, although the culture there is never earlier than Neolithic. From very early times there is evidence that a knowledge of domestication of animals existed and was practised. The most important species we have to consider in this connection are sheep, cattle, the pig, and perhaps the horse.

SHEEP (Plate 6)(5). In the wild state sheep and goats, both members of the subfamily *Caprinae*, are extremely alike and the true sheep (*Ovis*) has been differentiated, as such, from its relations when it has skull depressions in front of the orbits for scent glands and has glands between the toes of the hind as well as the fore feet. There exist to-day four types of wild sheep from which all our modern varieties seem to be descended. The first of these is the Mouflon (*Ovis musimon*) (Plate 6, no. 4). This type has a reddish brown coat with hair on the top and wool below; there is a dark dorsal band and the breast and forelimbs above the knee are also

Note chipped stone implement found in situ

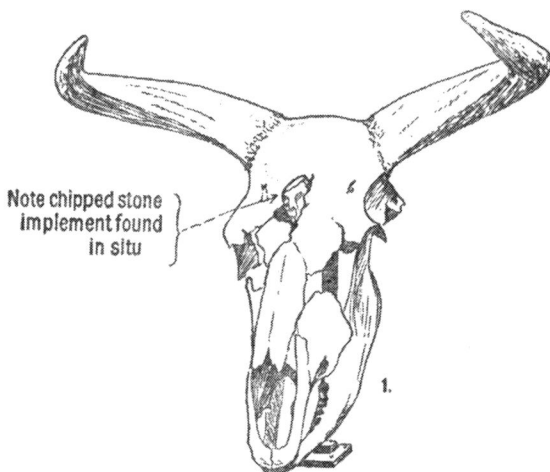

Plate 6. 1. Head of *Bos primigenius*. The animal had been killed with a stone implement. Now in the Sedgwick Museum at Cambridge.
2. Head of a Urial ram. 4. Head of a Mouflon ram.
3. Head of a Urial ewe. 5. Head of an Argali ram.

dark. Around the muzzle and eyes, inside the ears, on the buttocks and below the knees, the hair is white. Only the rams carry horns, which normally are curved backwards and outwards. The infraorbital pit is exceedingly shallow and the tail of negligible length. In Europe to-day the Mouflon is found in Sicily, Corsica, Sardinia, and Cyprus (*Ovis orientalis*); but in western Asia its varieties occur in Armenia, Persia, and on the south of the Elburz mountains, the range which bounds northern Persia and separates it from the Caspian Sea, running eastwards till it disappears in the sandy wastes of Russian Turkestan. This type was formerly found in the early Quaternary deposits of East Anglia and elsewhere, but seems to have become extinct by the end of Quaternary times. It is not certain where the Mouflon was first domesticated, but its descendants do not appear in the domesticated state in Europe till the very end of Neolithic, or more accurately, Copper Age times, when we find them as *Ovis aries studeri*, the large horned "Copper" sheep of the pile dwelling deposits of Lake Bienne, Switzerland.

The second type of wild sheep existing to-day is the Urial (*Ovis vignei*) (Plate 6, no. 2). In colour and appearance it is not unlike the Mouflon, although the colour is usually lighter, the summer coat being generally of a fawn shade. The rams have curved horns, and the ewes also have small goat-like horns (Plate 6, no. 3). The face pit is larger and deeper than that of the Mouflon. Representatives of this type range from north of the Elburz mountains to Tibet. It would seem that this variety was that first domesticated somewhere east of the Caspian Sea near the borders of Persia, as at Anau, and brought to Europe by the Neolithic invaders, for there seems no doubt that *Ovis aries palustris*, the

"Turbary" sheep of the Swiss lake dwellings is its descendant, belonging to the same race. Its bones, dug up from the lake deposits, agree substantially with those found in the later layers of Culture I excavated at Anau (see chapter III, p. 85). Later in the Bronze Age it met and was crossed with the Mouflon, by then introduced in a domesticated state into western Europe, and produced among other hybrid forms the four-horned sheep.

The third type of still existing wild sheep is the Argali (*Ovis ammon*) (Plate 6, no. 5). In the highlands of the Pamirs, in the Tien-Shan range, and the Altai mountains of Central Asia it still provides some of the most sporting and without doubt fascinating game-shooting possible. This sheep is of a very considerable size and is characterised by its long coiled horns. Outside Central Asia it no longer exists to-day, but the Merino and Norfolk Black Face are perhaps our nearest equivalents and doubtless contain Argali blood. An Argali-Urial hybrid seems to appear at Anau, but not until the end of the Neolithic Age. In England a very large sheep, probably of Argali stock, appears in the Bronze Age deposits of the Thames alluvium.

The fourth type still existing is the American Big-horn, but as this seems to have played no part in the European domestication and is exclusively a development of the New World we need not discuss it here.

It will thus be seen that in Neolithic Europe we are entirely concerned with *Ovis aries palustris*, the so-called "Turbary" sheep, which was of Urial stock and had been domesticated in the region now called Russian Turkestan and brought to Europe by the Neolithic invaders of the Eastern Area (see chapter V), who had a considerable share in the development of the earliest cultures of the Swiss lake dwellings, where the bones of this sheep are abundant in the deposits. Later we include *Ovis aries studeri* of Mouflon ancestry. From deposits of manure found it would seem that during the winter periods these sheep were kept in stables in the lake huts and fed on the products of agriculture. Both these varieties of sheep occurred in various parts of England during our periods.

GOATS. One variety of goat (*Capra hircus rütimeyeri*) has been identified in Switzerland, at Sutz and at Vinelz.

CATTLE(6). The Palaeolithic wild ox (*Bos primigenius*) (Plate 6, no. 1) continued to exist in Western Europe all through the changes of climate that took place at the end of Palaeolithic times. Unlike the bison this species was able to adapt itself to the new conditions, and in fact the last specimen was killed in the forests of Germany as late as the Middle Ages. But the first domesticated cattle that appear in the oldest lake dwellings of Neolithic date are quite unlike this wild European form and were almost certainly imported, possibly from Central Asia. They belong to the species *Bos taurus brachyceros* or, as it is more generally called, *Bos taurus longifrons*. They had comparatively short horns thus differing completely from *Bos primigenius* (the Urus), as well as being of altogether smaller build. At a later date, however, crossings took place with the old European variety, with the result that many hybrids were introduced. The remains of a hornless variety, *Bos taurus akeratos*, have also been found. Though the raising of cattle was practised in Neolithic times, it did not reach its height until well into the Early Metal Ages. As regards the two main species it is interesting to note, when travelling in Hungary, how the wide outspreading horns and big build of the oxen at the plough proclaim them descendants of the native Urus, while westwards our patient grazing cattle obviously owe more to the parentage of *Bos taurus longifrons*.

PIGS. The wild pig existed in Late Palaeolithic times, and was painted more than once, as for example the "galloping pig" on the ceiling at Altamira. But the so-called "Turbary" pig (*Sus scrofa palustris*), found in the Neolithic lake dwellings, is a much smaller animal with comparatively long legs; and once again, if we study the finds from Anau, we shall discover the origin of this domesticated form. *Sus scrofa domesticus* also occurs.

DOGS(7). The dog was the first animal to be domesticated—he naturally is of prime importance to man for purposes of protection and the herding of flocks. In Neolithic times we find firstly *Canis familiaris palustris*, a small variety, possibly of jackal descent. Later, but still of Neolithic date, are found the bones of *Canis familiaris matris optimae*, a larger wolf-like animal, probably an excellent sheep-dog[1]. His appearance at a time when the number of flocks of sheep was increasing is significant. *Canis intermedius*, a third type, has also been found, as well as another wolf-like variety, named *Inostranzewi*, that has been collected from Stone Age sites in Northern Europe and has been recognised at Lake Bienne in Switzerland.

HORSES(8). The origin of our modern horse has perhaps given rise to more investigation than that of any other domestic animal, but it is not intended to discuss the problem here at any length, as it seems to have played but a very small part in the life of our Neolithic forerunners. Perhaps this was owing to the difficulty of

---

[1] What are probably the remains of this dog have been observed at Anau in Culture 2.

domesticating it in pre-Metal Ages before effective bridles with bits could be manufactured. The original ancestor in Pliocene times was *Equus stenonis*. Four varieties are found in Quaternary times which Palaeolithic man seems to have hunted for food and drawn in the caves. These were, according to Cossar Ewart, the Steppe Horse (*Equus przewalskii*), the Plateau Horse (*Equus agilis*) including a northern "Celtic" and a southern "Libyan" variety, the Forest Horse (*Equus robustus*), and the fine-limbed *Equus sivalensis*. Only a small remnant of these Palaeolithic horses appear to have survived into Neolithic times, and as domestication hardly seems to have been practised, their use in the service of man does not seem to have been general till the Bronze Age.

Egypt with its rich early cultures and its teeming wild animal life only managed to domesticate two animals. The one was the ass, the other was the cat.

POTTERY

The influence of pottery on human existence, although less startling than that of agriculture and domestic animals, is by no means negligible. Instead of a fragment of a skull for a drinking cup and other purposes a new material was introduced that increased the possibility of refinement in the home. Its uses are innumerable, as any required shape can be readily obtained. Further it provides a surface that simply calls for decoration, and it is fairly safe to say that it is not till the introduction of pottery that we get anything that can be described as art for art's sake on a large scale. The pottery of Middle Minoan times (Middle Bronze Age) in Crete dates from a moment at the very end of our period or even outside it, but anyone faced with the

wonderful decoration of this pottery as seen, for example, in the Museum at Candia, is astounded at the
progress in comfort and refinement made by mankind
since Palaeolithic times, and even if we go to the
opposite extreme and examine the so-called Spiral
Meander pottery of some of the first comers into
eastern Europe who had a truly Neolithic civilisation,
we are amazed at the power over their medium and the
skill in decoration displayed. Of course the old Upper
Palaeolithic hunter in the depth of his cave temple
remains unsurpassed in the beauty, skill and naturalism
of his drawing, but it should be remembered that in this
case it was not art for art's sake but for very definite
utilitarian sympathetic magic purposes. The invention
of pottery did a great deal to promote the use of art,
whether painting or engraving, for decorative purposes.

Many people have claimed that Palaeolithic man
was not without a knowledge of pottery technique, that
is to say, of burning plastic clay to produce a hard substance. Examples of fragments of so-called pottery have
been cited from a few Palaeolithic sites, especially in
Belgium, but, apart from the fact that the lack of available evidence necessitates caution when it is remembered how often objects of much later date occur
out of their place in a wrong *milieu*, the occasional
burning of a piece of clay in the camp or home
fire and the production of a fragment of what might
be described as pottery is by no means impossible.
Before Palaeolithic pottery can be really admitted, un-
deniable finds of intentionally shaped pots or other
objects from Palaeolithic layers must be recognised.
Even a pot shaped out of clay and then sun-dried does
not constitute true pottery and might have been manufactured at any moment in man's history. True pottery

involves careful and scientific firing of the shaped material so as to produce a smooth hard object.

Clay, if used alone for pot making, may contract and crack when fired, or if on the other hand it is too greasy, although it does not dry and crack, it may fail to keep its shape when burnt. It was soon found that the clay material must be mixed with something to render it porous, so that the steam formed when it is heated may readily escape. The most usual materials used from early times were sand or other micaceous matter, and it was not long before it was discovered that charcoal, made from burnt wood or bones, is another very useful substance for this purpose, and that clay with such admixture produces a pot, which, when fired, has a surface that can be easily burnished. Most clays naturally contain a small proportion of iron salts in their composition, and if they are fired in the open hearth with free access of air these iron salts get oxidised and the result is a red-coloured pot. If, however, free air is kept away oxidisation does not take place and the resulting colour is grey, or, if charcoal has been used to mix with the clay, black.

It seems that a pot with a smooth surface was always the ideal, and the early folk of the Danube river basin obtained this end by using only very carefully prepared materials containing no hard lumps. The result of this good paste is a pottery that it is a joy to handle to-day. But good paste requires a lot of preparation and the raw material is not always readily obtainable, and so there followed the invention of what is known as "slip." Here the pot is modelled of comparatively coarse material and allowed to dry. It is then dipped in a thin paste of the fine material reduced to the consistency of very thick soup; the fine paste adheres to the coarse material of the pot in the form of a thin film; the whole is then fired. A vessel so made has, as it were, a veneer, often exceedingly thin, giving it a fine smooth surface, though underneath it is made of the coarse, easily obtained paste.

Among modern primitive peoples to-day pots are shaped not only by hollowing out a ball of clay with the hand, but also by rolling the clay into a sort of elongated sausage with which the pot is built up corkscrew wise by twisting this sausage into concentric rings. This method, however, does not seem ever to have been employed by Neolithic man in Europe. The potter's wheel was not introduced until well into the Bronze Age.

Nothing will be said here as to the decoration of pottery in Neolithic and Early Metal Ages, as this will be treated of separately in chapter IV.

THE GRINDING AND POLISHING
OF STONE TOOLS

The only method employed by our Palaeolithic fore-runners for the shaping of their stone tools had been flaking and chipping. In some cases the tool was formed by chipping off flakes in all directions until the tool required had been finally fashioned. In other cases a large flake already removed from a block of flint was chosen, and this in turn trimmed and flaked to the required shape. It is obvious that not every kind of stone is suitable for these operations; a coarse-grained granite, for instance, will not flake evenly, and it is almost impossible to produce anything like a satis-factory edge by chipping alone. Practically speaking, the only suitable rock is flint as this can be flaked readily and evenly. Flint is a hydrated silica and is of common occurrence in chalk where it often occurs in bands or layers, the formation of which still remains obscure, although in some cases it is seen to be due to the action of lowly organisms. The flint, being resistant, remains when the softer limestone has been weathered away, and so it is common to find layers of flint covering large areas where chalk formerly existed but has since been completely denuded. Flint can be readily flaked by percussion or by pressure, that is, by striking a blow or by applying pressure at a given point, so setting up a fracture system, and thus removing a tiny flake, leaving a flat flake facet. The intersection of such facets readily yields a fine edge of extreme sharpness—certainly as sharp as an ordinary bluntish penknife. Tools made from flint have however one great disadvantage; although a sharp edge can be easily obtained it is exceedingly brittle, and anything like continuous use for hard or tough work is impossible. Man of the Neolithic civilisation discovered that an edge could also be obtained by a process of grinding or polishing or both, and on other materials than flint. The result was the obtaining of a sharp edge on such rocks as diorite or even on a fine-grained granite; an edge which had the quality of toughness as well as sharpness. The method employed was simple; all that was required was a flat slab of hard sandstone up and down which the stone to be sharpened could be worked in exactly the same way as our own metal chisels are sharpened on a stone to-day. The importance of this discovery was very considerable, as for the first time carpentry came within man's grasp. In former days under the climatic conditions of Quaternary times trees were often scarce, and Palaeolithic man had little incentive to skill in woodwork, but with the change of climate and the growth of forests the utilisation of this readily workable material became a matter of great importance. A ground and polished stone axe was still not very suitable for the working of hard woods, and such trees were still as a rule spared from the service of man until metal came into regular use[1]; but softer woods, like the fir and the spruce, are readily amenable to the stone axe. As long ago as 1879 a number of prehistorians in Denmark made experiments with Neolithic stone axes and found that forest fir trees could be felled and worked without the aid of any other tool, and as late as our own day there have been primitive peoples who were capable of manufacturing dug-out canoes of immense length and beautiful finish without any other than stone tools. But it must, of course, be remembered that even though Neolithic man had learnt the advantage of grinding and polishing an edge on his stone axes, the old method of flaking was by no means abandoned, and the student must beware of assigning an implement or an industry to an older culture simply because of the absence of any grinding or polishing. Although flint itself is sometimes prepared in this way to obtain a sharp edge, and although the process of polishing does produce a certain toughening, yet when a sharp cutting edge on flint was required it still remained easier and more efficient to obtain that edge by the older methods of flaking. Grinding and polishing being a slow process, the heavy, rough, chopper-like tools of everyday life would often be roughly fashioned from nodular flints by flaking, as it would hardly be worth while to go to the trouble of the lengthy process of grinding and polishing. Again, it must be remembered that for the grinding and

[1] Occasionally objects made of oak have been found and perhaps too some of the piles of the Lake Neuchâtel Neolithic villages were made of this material.

polishing of tools slabs of sandstone of suitable lengths were necessary, and that in many areas, as, for example, in East Anglia in our own country, sandstone does not exist naturally. Where this was the case either the "grind-stone" or the finished article was imported from elsewhere. As this was a difficult matter in these early times, when commercial routes were not yet organised, we often find the curious phenomenon of a ground and polished axe, become blunt and worn with use, that has been re-sharpened at a much later date by the older flaking methods. In the perfectly made ground and polished tool the whole surface of the object is smoothed and polished, but there was also a "cheaper variety" where only the actual working edge was ground and polished and the body of the tool was formed by the easier flaking method. Thus it sometimes happens that the prehistorian has to determine in a given instance whether the flaking of the tool was prior to or contemporary with the polishing, or whether the flaking was long posterior and of the nature of re-sharpening and re-shaping; this is by no means always easy.

MINES. Raw material for tool-making was, of course, of the utmost importance, and, roughly speaking, may be divided into two categories: (1) rocks suitable for grinding and polishing into axes or celts, and (2) flint capable of being readily chipped into small sharp knife blades, awls, scrapers, or into rough, heavy, chopper-like tools. For the first of these a fine-grained igneous rock was required, and at Penmaenmawr, Wales, for example, a quarry site has been discovered where blocks of the greenish grey rock obtained were first roughly shaped by flaking processes, until a more or less desired form was obtained, and then for the most part exported elsewhere to be finally ground and polished. But the occurrence of suitable igneous rock is so common in certain parts of our own country and in Europe, that the concentration into definite manufactory sites would seem to have been hardly necessary. The material was easy to hand and could be worked up into tools almost anywhere in these favoured districts. With flint, however, this is not always the case, and suitable natural deposits are much less frequent. Again, although flint often occurs on the surface, washed out of the chalk or left when the chalk itself has been washed completely away, the greatest quantity of this material is found in the form of nodules occurring in bands in the chalk or limestone; and so, from Neolithic times onwards, there grew up a flint-mining industry; two or three such mines have been studied in our own country as well as some abroad. As we shall mention the most famous of these—Grimes Graves—in a later chapter, it might be more convenient to take now a foreign example, such as St Gertrude in Maestricht(10), south-east Holland, on the borders of Belgium. Here bands containing flints occur in the chalk and were reached by means of vertical shafts, sometimes twenty feet or so in depth, and horizontal passages communicating with the base of the shafts were dug out. Blocks of chalk were left at intervals to hold up the roof of these galleries, which were constructed in quite a scientific manner. The implements employed—the miner's bag of tools—were naturally specialised and consisted among other things of picks made from stag's antler. The flint was brought to the surface in the form of large nodules which were at once roughly worked by flaking processes into the shapes required; this was, of course, to avoid having to transport a useless weight of material. When an area served by a shaft, and its attendant galleries at the bottom, was exhausted, the rubbish from these workings was thrown back into the pits, and to-day at St Gertrude we find them almost completely filled up with such rejected fragments.

A pathetic note is struck at a flint mine at Spiennes in Belgium. A miner seems to have gone into a gallery with his little son when the roof fell in killing them both. However, they now have the honour to repose in a glass case at the National Museum at Brussels.

Neolithic industries will be more particularly described in their due place, but in general the reader should remember that the only tools that have survived are those that were made from imperishable material, and that such things as wooden tools have not been preserved. It is not therefore fair to judge of an industry or compare it with others when we have only a portion of that industry remaining. This should be specially borne in mind in the case of Neolithic civilisation, when the forest growth around was continually inviting the use of this abundant and easily worked material.

BIBLIOGRAPHY AND REFERENCES

(1) D. VIOLLIER and OTHERS. "Pfahlbauten." *Mitt. der Antiq. Gesell. in Zürich*, Band XXIX, Heft 4, 1924.

(2) M. HOERNES. *Die Neolithische Station von Butmir*. Vienna, 1895.

(3) See bibliography (2) at end of chapter 1.

(4) R. PUMPELLY. *Explorations in Turkestan*, published by the Carnegie Institution in 3 volumes—the first in 1905, the other two in 1908.

(5) J. COSSAR EWART. "Domestic Sheep and their Wild Ancestors," two papers, one 1913 the other 1914, in the *Trans. of the Highland and Agricult. Soc. of Scotland*.

R. LYDEKKER. *The Sheep and his Cousins*. 1912.

(6) R. LYDEKKER. *The Ox and its Kindred*. 1911.

J. COSSAR EWART. *The animal remains at Newstead*, incorporated with *A Roman frontier post and its people*, by J. Curle, Glasgow, 1911.

(7) T. STUDER. Article in the *Zoologischer Anzeiger*, Band XXIX, Heft 1, p. 24, June 1905.

(8) R. LYDEKKER. *The Horse and its relatives*. 1912.
J. COSSAR EWART. "The Multiple Origin of Horses and Ponies." *Trans. of the Highland and Agricult. Soc. of Scotland.* 1904.

(9) H. WARREN. "A Stone-Axe Factory at Graig-Cwyd, Penmaenmawr." *Journ. Roy. Anth. Inst.* vol. xlix, July–Dec. 1919.

(10) M. DE PUYDT. A short account will be found with bibliography in the *Bull. de l'Inst. arch. liégeois*, tome XL, 1910.
See also Miss LAYARD. "Excavations on the Neolithic site of Sainte-Gertrude." *Proc. Prehist. Soc. of E. Anglia*, vol. v, pt 1, 1925.

CHAPTER III

NEOLITHIC CIVILISATION (*contd.*)

HAVING briefly described the Neolithic civilisation and the effect of certain new discoveries on human existence, it is now necessary to turn to the climatic conditions under which Neolithic man lived and then attempt to trace his origin and describe his homes.

CLIMATE

The various changes of climate that took place in post-Glacial times have of late been more and more studied and their importance more and more realised [1]. Mankind was formerly almost completely at the mercy of climate, and it is not till comparatively recent times that he has been enabled to exist tolerably under adverse conditions. Post-Glacial changes of climate are undoubtedly of considerably less intensity and differ to a certain extent from those of Quaternary times, but none the less they have played an extremely important rôle in human history. In thinking of climate two things must be remembered: the first is temperature, the second is humidity. We were most concerned with the former when considering Palaeolithic times, but it is the latter to which we must now turn our attention. A warm, dry climate, for example, is not favourable to forest growth, which is especially stimulated by a warm, damp atmosphere. This alone is an important factor in human history, for even with ground and polished tools mankind would hardly be able to make much headway against the growth of forests as a whole; in fact it will be seen, when distribution maps for such an area as our own country are studied, that clay forest-bearing lands were not inhabited by Neolithic man. When, however, these forests dwindled, owing to changes of climate, the virgin ground would at once be occupied. Neolithic man had not harnessed nature by means of a steam saw; to a large extent he was necessarily under her control. Again, with warm damp conditions would come an increase of fens and morasses, breeding fever and other diseases, and although Neolithic man may have been more resistant to disease than we are to-day, there is no reason to think that he was any more able to cope with such a thing as an epidemic of malaria, than the modern peasant of the north coast of Crete or any other fever-stricken spot. Neolithic man had no Burroughs and Welcome's quinine pills, nor did he possess any paraffin or the knowledge that a barrel of it poured on a morass will kill mosquito larvae and so prevent future fever! Even in our own days we are hardly able to snap our fingers at nature in respect of disease, and our forebears had neither the means nor the knowledge for coping with it.

As has been seen in chapter I, the Mesolithic Period was ushered in by a catastrophic change of temperature, when the climate over large parts of Northern Europe suddenly became warm and dry and the old almost Arctic conditions of Upper Palaeolithic times disappeared, along with the old fauna. The reindeer left Germany never to return; everywhere the glaciers withdrew, in Norway almost to their present limits. Forests spread rapidly, especially birch and fir, and the water-levels in lakes shrank back. In this connection the conditions of the Federsee, a small lake near Buchau in Württemberg, have been specially studied and it seems that at this period the water-level was very low indeed and only the muddy detritus is found. Bogs dried up, peat was formed and loess deposited—all circumstances pointing to a climate probably warmer and drier in summer than ours is to-day. Towards the end of this "Boreal" period, as it has been called, oaks appeared in greater quantities, coinciding with the sinking of the Baltic Sea and we find ourselves in the "Atlantic" period when, though still warm, it was very damp. This, even more than the "Boreal" period, was the hey-day of the forests of Central Europe. They flourished exceedingly, and as a result the only human cultures we find at this time are the peripheral ones of late Mesolithic type. In drier places firs were predominant, but the oak and spruce were the main forest trees. On the alps *Rhododendron ferrugineum* replaced the larch. Lake levels rose, bogs increased, so-called "atlantic" plants like *Hereda*, *Taxus*, and *Abies* spread rapidly and Weber says the "older" Sphagnum peats were now laid down in the North German moors. It has been suggested that in South Sweden the annual rainfall must have been forty inches at least.

But later again, in full Neolithic and Bronze Age times the land rose once more and renewed dryness set in. We have now entered a climatic optimum known as the Sub-Boreal period. Forests began to thin, water-levels fell, the Bodensee and Federsee were once more very low; bogs, including those of Ireland, dried up, heaths took their place, trees grew where before Sphagnum flourished, surface springs failed, and desiccation layers are found, for example at Ravensburg (Württemberg) and at Pullenhofen on the Moosach, a stream of the Inn system. Loess was once more deposited, warmth-loving water-plants, such as *Najas marina* and *Trapa natans*, abounded, and it has been concluded that the summer temperature reached its post-Glacial maximum. These conditions lasted till the climate again deteriorated in the Early Iron Age (a period outside our present study) and this deterioration may have been in part responsible for the movements of peoples which then took place.

Such climatic changes as these of course took place gradually and their full effect would not be felt at once. For instance in the Sub-Boreal time, although the forests began to thin with the increasing dryness, they were not penetrable to man till the end of Neolithic times.

As has been indicated, the evidence for these climatic changes is obtained from a study of moorlands, heaths and peat-lands and the plants that go to make their composition. There is often a stratigraphical superposition that can be determined, and correlation with human industries is possible when definite recognisable cultures are found in certain layers. Our knowledge, however, is still imperfect and much further work is required. Although in early times these climatic changes were doubtless the largest factor determining migrations of people and the like, at later dates, although they still played their part, other factors were introduced, and the student must keep a sense of proportion and not be led away into considering, as has been suggested by more than one author, that the history of the wanderings of people up to mediaeval times can be completely interpreted in terms of climatic changes. It must be remembered that what we have said of climatic changes in northern Europe as a whole does not preclude local variations. For instance in the Boreal Period the British Isles were for the most part, thanks to Atlantic Cyclonic depressions, having a far damper climate and bogs were being formed. South-eastern England escaped, and enjoyed the continental warmth and dryness.

Further the Pyrenean districts of the south of France, outside the area already described, also seem to have had a warm, damp climate in Mesolithic times if the quantity of snail shells in the Azilian deposits can be taken as a guide.

There is one area of the earth's surface of special importance to us here in Europe, and that is Central Asia, for it is here that we have to look for the origin of much of our Neolithic culture. The matter is intimately intermixed with questions of climate so that it will not be out of place to consider it at this point.

Central Asia to-day contains some of the loftiest mountains in the world and some of the largest deserts. It is an inland area without any access to the sea, and what precipitation and rainfall there is drains to no ocean, but is either engulfed in the sands or evaporated into the air. In Quaternary times, however, a very different state of affairs existed. Over a large area now desert there stretched a huge inland ocean, of which the Caspian, the Aral, Lake Balkash, and many another small sheet of water are to-day the shrivelled remains. This inland ocean had communication also with the Black Sea, as at that time the water level of what is now the Caspian Sea stood something like 600 feet higher(3). The influence of this large sheet of water, fed from glacier streams due to the melting of the ice sheets of the end of Quaternary times, was naturally enormous. Large sheets of water not only act as a governor on temperature, holding the warmth of a warm period, thus preventing the temperature getting too hot, and giving it out again during a cold season, thus preventing the temperature getting too low; but also the evaporation and subsequent precipitation from such a great expanse of sea produced the moisture necessary to make large areas of Central Asia, which are now desert, fertile and fruitful lands. We therefore have to consider the likelihood that towards the end of Quaternary times when western Europe was not the most suitable place on earth for human habitation, Central Asia, in spite of the possession of high glacier-covered ranges and mountains, was far more favourably situated. But the dryness that set in in post-Glacial times, and more especially it would seem during Mesolithic times, while it considerably bettered the situation in western Europe, brought untold ruin to mankind in Central Asia. Doubtless, too, this was augmented by earth movements, by the opening of the Bosphorus, and by the draining and disappearance of the great central Asian sea. Man was faced with either extinction or migration and he apparently chose the latter alternative; hence from this time we find in Europe a continual pressure from the east. Whether we are to look to Central Asia for the cradle of agriculture and domestic animals, pottery, and all the other things that go to make up our modern civilisation we may never know. The desert holds its secrets. It may be that we ought to look still further eastwards remembering that the arid stretches of the great Gobi Desert must at one time have yielded fertile land for mankind's herds and crops. The recent discovery of painted pottery of Neolithic or Early Metal Age in northern China(2)—not to speak of the earlier Palaeolithic industries—may have an important bearing on this question; but there is as yet no evidence whatsoever to show whether the movements of Neolithic man were westwards from China, to Central Asia, and thence to Europe, or whether—as seems more likely to the author—the movement was eastwards as well as westwards from the intermediate cradle of Central Asia.

But if we are to look to Central Asia as the source of our modern civilisation we must examine its geography in more detail. Although the desert areas hold, and may perhaps for ever hold, their secrets, the main outlines of the geography of the district do not seem to have changed with the deterioration of climate. There is no evidence for any earth movement on a large scale since Neolithic times, and a note on the geography of the area may help clear thinking in respect to possible movements of peoples.

Suppose that a student could go up to an incredible height in an aeroplane and see, laid as a map under his feet, the whole of Asia and Europe. He would observe that, except in the extreme east where the plains of China allow free passage north and south, Asia can be divided into a northern and a southern area (Plate 7). The backbone is formed by some of the highest mountains in the world. To the east lies the high plateau of Tibet bounded to the northwards by the still higher Kuen Lun mountains that border the southern edge of the Tarim basin and the now desert Chinese Turkestan. These high ranges north of Tibet merge into the great Karakoram range, the Hindu Kush, and the main massif of the Pamirs. To the south of Tibet arise the Himalayas and the Trans-Himalayas. To the north the Pamirs link with the Tien-Shan range or Celestial Mountains, which ultimately run along the northern edge of Chinese Turkestan and vanish into the Gobi Desert near the oasis of Hami. Westwards of the Pamirs the mountains slope away into the deserts of Russian Turkestan, and at this point there is an important gap between the mountains just described that

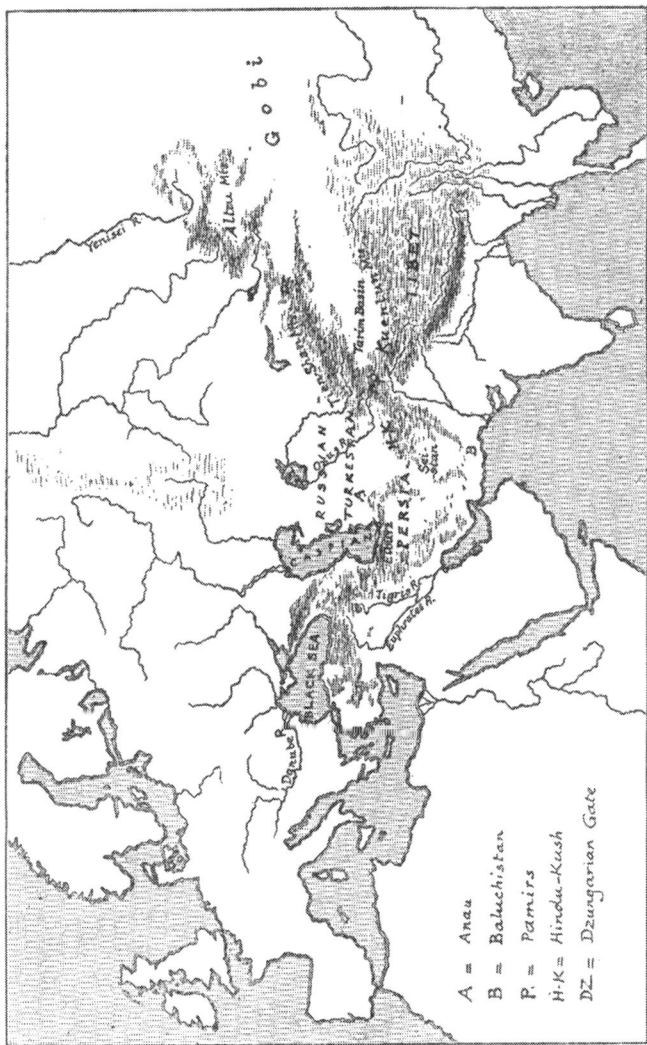

A = Anau
B = Baluchistan
P = Pamirs
H-K = Hindu-Kush
DZ = Dzungarian Gate

Plate 7. Sketch map showing physical geography of Central Asia.

form an almost impassable barrier for mankind between
north and south, and the Elburz Mountains that border
the southern shore of the Caspian Sea and in turn link
on with the very difficult mountain masses of the
Caucasus area and Asia Minor. Between the two
Turkestans, over the Pamirs where they join the Tien-
Shan range to the north, there has been a passage for
human intercourse east and westwards since immemorial
antiquity. The main pass is the watershed between the
upper waters of the Tarim, that to-day disappear in the
sandy waste of Lob-Nor in Chinese Turkestan, and the
head waters of the Oxus basin, that to-day get no further
than the Aral Sea. Over this pass, B.C. 200, were taken
the coloured silks from China that delighted the Greek
world, and the woven tapestry that travelled eastwards
in exchange. Even then the climate of Chinese Turkestan was very different from that of to-day, as is shown by
the work of Sir Aurel Stein, who has also collected from
this area stone implements the culture and age of which
have not yet been determined. They may possibly be
connected with some other early industries discovered
in Mongolia and the Gobi Desert which are in all
probability of Neolithic date. The Tien-Shan range,
which runs east and west just north of the Pamirs, is
joined by mountain masses running north-eastwards
that link it with the various Altai groups. These
mountain masses are pierced by a very important,
although extremely narrow, gap that again allows
intercourse between east and west; this is the so-called
Dzungarian Gate which to-day connects the plains of
Siberia with the desert area of Dzungaria, a continuation
of the great Gobi Desert. In the Middle Ages when
the "Mongol" hordes around the Gobi Desert were
beginning to expand and feel their strength this passage

was of great importance. At one point the Altai group north-east of the Dzungarian Gate, stretching up past Lake Baikal, divides in two and encloses a large inland area as yet little known. Here are the head waters of the great Yenisei River that breaks through the mountains in the famous pass called the Kempchik Bom. In this region there still live to-day primitive hunters with flocks of tame reindeer, men who until recently used only the bow and arrow, now replaced, through the agency of Siberian traders, by the more modern firearm.

To a certain extent, then, Central Asia is connected with the vast stretches of the Gobi Desert, which are in turn linked on without interruption with the plains of China and of Chinese Turkestan. The main connecting passages are over the Pamirs and down the Oxus valley into Russian Turkestan, or through the Dzungarian Gate direct into the Siberian plains.

South of the mountains to the west of the Hindu Kush there exist to-day other great desert areas— Seistan and Iran generally—and these communicate without undue difficulty with the northern plains of India. The only easy connection, however, between these large desert areas to the south and the northern regions is through the gap of Russian Turkestan.

Continuing westward, the backbone, including the mountains of Georgia and Caucasia generally and those of Asia Minor, ends with the Black and Aegean Seas. The desert areas of Iran and Persia are to a certain extent cut off by mountain chains from the fertile lands watered by the Euphrates and Tigris, but these mountain chains can be passed or readily turned. Beyond lie deserts and the coastal lands of Syria and Palestine which form one limb of a fertile horseshoe-shaped area running thence into Mesopotamia which forms the other limb.

Westward again lies the open sea, not readily traversed until a later date when the art of navigation had been properly discovered. Southwards, along what is now the north coast of Africa, and down the Nile valley, communication by water would be an easier matter. At only one other point besides the Russian Turkestan gap could migrations from the southern (now desert) areas influence Europe, and that is at the narrow passage of the Dardanelles.

It would seem probable therefore that the migrations that gave rise to the Early Neolithic cultures of Europe came from areas north of the main backbone already described, influenced more or less from the southern area through the comparatively narrow Russian Turkestan gap, while Syria, Mesopotamia and Egypt derived their different, if analogous, early cultures rather from the southern areas[1]. By Early Metal Age times mankind had become more skilful and more venturesome, probably with the rise of commerce; many of the simpler mountain ranges were traversed, and we find the influence of such a centre of culture as Mesopotamia spreading far and wide. It must also be remembered that with the continual drying process that set in towards the latter half of Neolithic times, mountain masses, hitherto impassable owing to snow and glaciers, now became free and open. We note from this date the beginning of the use of the Brenner Pass for bringing the Beaker pots of Italy to the folk of what is now Bohemia; and at a slightly later date the amber of the Baltic to the shores of the Mediterranean.

One of the few sites that have been investigated in Central Asia is Anau, a delta-oasis now situated close to the Central Asian Railway, not far from Astrabad. It

---

[1] Sir Flinders Petrie has lately sought to prove that the earliest Egyptians came from the southern Caucasus.

lies to the north of a small range of mountains that to some extent occupy part of the Russian Turkestan gap that we have already alluded to. Two mounds (or kurgans, as they are called) were investigated at the beginning of the present century by an American expedition under the direction of Raphael Pumpelly(3). These mounds were formed by successive human habitations, each new generation building on the ruins of the former. Four different and successive cultures were discovered and the following account gives a very brief résumé of the finds. It is interesting to note that wheat and barley, denoting agriculture, appear before the domestication of animals.

CULTURE I (*Earliest*)

Handmade painted ware, geometric designs only.

Cultivation of wheat (*Triticum vulgare*) and barley (*Hordeum distichum*).

Rectangular houses of air-dried bricks.

Flint awls and flakes, mace heads of stone, bone awls.

Spindle whorls, milling stones, turquoise beads.

Some evidence of the existence of copper and lead.

Children buried in contracted position under the houses.

At first, during early centuries only, wild animals such as ox, sheep, gazelle, deer, horse, fox, wolf, probably hunted for food.

Later local domestication of ox (*Bos nomadicus*), pig (*Sus palustris*, the turbary pig), horse (doubtfully domesticated), and sheep. Of the two varieties of sheep one was large-horned, while the other, the turbary sheep, is not found till towards the end of this period.

Note absence of: potter's wheel, gold, silver, tin, celts, arrow heads, lapis lazuli, dog, camel, and goat.

CULTURE II

Similar to I but showing in addition:

Polychrome painted ware.

Bottomless earthenware bake-oven pots, pivotal door stones, flint sickles, sling stones, copper pins, lapis lazuli and cornelian beads.

Domestic animals now include: short-horned oxen, camels, the dog, and hornless sheep.

Note continued absence of: potter's wheel, gold, silver, bronze, arrow heads, celts, etc.

CULTURE III

Similar to above but showing addition of:

Potter's wheel and furnace, and some incised pottery.

Alloying with tin and lead appears, also arrow heads made of copper, stone and obsidian.

Terra-cotta figurines (comp. Butmir) of goddesses, bulls, cows, etc., are found.

Note continued absence of: stone or metal celts or burnt bricks. Still no iron or glazed or incrusted ware present.

CULTURE IV

Iron used and therefore outside our subject.

Practically speaking this is the only site in this most important area that has been at all properly investigated, we cannot therefore build too much theory upon it; it is to be hoped that, when political circumstances permit, continued investigation may be undertaken and further work accomplished. Mr Pumpelly attempted to establish an absolute chronology for these cultures, mainly by consideration of the growth of the mounds and so on. Naturally this is an exceedingly difficult proposition, and there is no reason to assume that the rate of growth of the material was constant. It is probable that the estimate of ten thousand years ago for the earliest culture is considerably too high.

HABITATIONS

A word or two must be said as to the actual Neolithic houses and habitations. These may roughly be divided into three series: (1) Land habitations, (2) Pile dwellings, (3) Cave homes.

LAND HABITATIONS

The floor of the hut consisting of dried mud, or in loess lands of compressed loam, was often partially sunk in the ground. It was often surrounded by large boulders which supported the wall and roof beams. Wattle and daub work filled the interstices between the wooden framework. Huts were usually congregated together to form definite villages and these were sometimes placed in sites well chosen for defence and even fortified with ramparts. In the prehistoric villages each house or group of houses generally possessed what is known as a food pit. This consists as a rule of a funnel-shaped shaft some two or three yards deep and in it provisions were probably stored. The food pit is found still in villages of as late a date as the Early Iron Age, if not later. It is rather depressing for the excavator who was hoping that he was dealing with a Neolithic food pit, to come across, after hours of patient work, an Early Iron Age chisel from near its very bottom!

As a typical example of one of these Neolithic homes we may take a Belgian *fond de cabane*(4). Let us join a party of exploration from Liège to the Hesbayen plateau. In all directions spread ploughed fields. The leader of the party is armed with a long thin staff something over a metre long and ending in a sort of corkscrew. Every now and then in suitable places where *fonds de cabanes* have been reported this staff is plunged into the ground and then carefully withdrawn. The corkscrew end is then examined; if the fragments of earth brought up on it are merely the ordinary soil there is nothing to hope for on excavation at that point. If, on the other hand, a certain amount of black cinder material is seen with the earth then we are in the middle of an old

Neolithic house. Excavation is started from that point down to a depth at which the cinder layer is reached; then continued carefully to right and left to determine the exterior walls of the hut emplacement, which in the case of these Belgian *fonds de cabanes* are always buried a foot or two in the ground. On being excavated the hut emplacement is usually found to be circular or oval, besides being somewhat splayed, so that the diameter is wider at the top than at the bottom. The sinking of the hut emplacement in the ground was no doubt due to the added warmth thereby gained, and also to the fact that a lower roof would be needed; naturally this would only be possible in dry areas, such as the high Hesbayen plateau, as in low lands such hutments would be continually water-logged. A hearth marked out with stones occurs within the hutment as well as tools, pots and other household furniture. Occasionally it is found that not a home but a workshop hut has been excavated, and here pottery is for the most part absent, while blocks of flint, nuclei, finished and unfinished tools, and fragments flaked off abound. That the roofs of these hutments were formed of joist-like beams with a sort of wattle and daub filling the inter-stices is attested by the finding now and then of frag-ments of clay which have fallen on the hearth and been burnt hard, but still bear the imprint of the twigs and small boughs on which they had been smeared.

Elsewhere in Europe still more complicated and well-built rectangular houses, sometimes with an internal division, are found, especially towards the end of Neo-lithic times. The store pit and, of course, the hearth, are the chief features. Corner posts with a varying number of intermediate wall posts supported the roof. Near Mayen in the Rhine province of Germany three or four such "post-houses" were found in a row of which the middle two, having a common wall, seem to form a two-roomed house. The larger of these two rooms had a central post to support the peak of the roof; such a central post being of quite frequent occurrence. Later it appears that sometimes an outer row of posts helped to support the wide overhanging roof thus making a veranda or passage on two sides of the house. Of Passage Grave times (see chapter VI) are a few horseshoe-shaped houses built of thick wicker-work and plaster between widely separated posts. Sometimes a stone table or seat appears in a fairly central position, the hearth being in the wide opening. Can we in this connection compare the Chambered tomb at St Nicholas near Cardiff which has a dry-walling in front forming a horseshoe-shaped perron in front of the tomb? Many people see in the great grave constructions only "soul-houses." At Haldorf, near Melsungen (Hesse Cassel) is a small model house of megaron form having a nearly square inner room and a narrow forecourt with immense corner posts. Goessler describes a two-storied rect-angular house from the Neolithic village of Gross-gartach near Heilbronn in Württemberg in which the upper room in the angle of the roof was apparently used as a sleeping place. The Beaker folk in the Spanish peninsula, France and England seem to have built round houses of from 3·5 to 5·25 metres diameter, necessitating a central support. Only one example of this type has yet been found in Germany, i.e. at Oltingen. Of Late Neolithic date in South Russia is found the "Zemljanka" or earth-house of the Tripolje culture (see chapter V). It consists generally of an oblong pit surrounded by an earth wall which is roofed in. In the middle a smaller deeper pit is dug where is the hearth below a smoke hole. A sort of raised sleeping bench runs all round, reached by earthen steps. Stone Age finds in Bulgaria show a similar earth-house with fire-hardened and sometimes painted walls. In Thessaly, at Dimini and Sesklo, we meet once more the megaron form in which the slight prolongation of the long walls makes a sort of outer court. The hearth is in the inner room and sometimes there are one or more further rooms built out at the back. These megaron houses belong to Period II in Thessaly when the culture is closely allied to, if not identical with, the important "painted pottery" culture which invaded Europe at the end of the Neolithic and the beginning of the Copper Age.

Small pottery models of houses were sometimes made and are found in the deposits. A well-made example can be seen in the museum at Brno (=Brunn) (Plate 29, fig. 4).

When these land habitations were gathered into regular villages, something of the nature of paved streets are occasionally found. Several such villages, dating from various periods of the Neolithic Age, have been excavated, for example, in Lower Austria. Often there seems to have been a courtyard just outside the house, which cannot have been very different in appearance from many of the small farmhouses of the same district to-day. In these a more or less small courtyard is generally surrounded on three sides by bungalow buildings (with at most a loft), comprising living, sleeping and kitchen quarters, as well as sheds for the pigs and the stock. In the courtyard is the pump, and from it often radiate narrow paved paths to the kitchen and elsewhere. The whole thing is far less straggly than our own farm yards and has a much more compact appearance.

PILE DWELLINGS

The lake or pile dwellings were developed in certain districts with an eye to safety both from attacks of hostile humans as well as wild animals. For their growth suitable conditions were necessary, and although in Metal Age times, especially in the Iron Age, their existence has been proved over a wide area in Europe, in Neolithic times they are for the most part restricted to the comparatively narrow belt of country forming the lower slopes of the Alps. They are common, for example, in Switzerland round Lake Neuchâtel, the Lake of Lucerne, and the Lake of Constance, and are found right along until the mountains disappear into the plains of Hungary. On the other side of the hills have been found what are called the Italian lake dwellings, and others also occur along the Julian Alps, as is testified by their presence near Loubliana (Laibach)— a site or rather sites of extreme richness that have yielded Late Neolithic objects of great beauty, but which are as yet but imperfectly studied and excavated.

The existence of these pile dwellings was first recognised as long ago as 1853 during chance excavations on the shore of one of the Swiss lakes at a time when, owing to the dry season, the water was standing especially low, the piles themselves being uncovered and the whole matter investigated by Keller. The piles consist of blocks of wood varying from 3 to 9 inches in diameter and from 15 to 30 feet long, generally roughly pointed and driven into the ground along the shallow edge of the lake or more probably into the marshy margins. On these piles rested cross beams, forming a platform on which the houses were built. As many as fifty thousand of these piles have been noted at a single site. Connection with the mainland was kept up by means of a narrow causeway, which could readily be destroyed in time of danger. The Neolithic lake dwellings are quite close to the shore, but in Early Metal Age times they were often built over the water at a considerable distance from the land. Naturally not every lake is suitable to have pile dwellings round its shores. A mountain lake with rocky bottom would obviously be unsuitable; what is required is a comparatively large sheet of water with a wide shallow margin and a muddy or peaty bottom. Such conditions occur *par excellence* near Loubliana in the Julian Alps, where there is an immense mountain plain, which has now become moor, owing to infilling brought down by glacial streams from the surrounding ranges, but which was formerly an immense sheet of shallow water, the overflow of which was carried off by the River Save. The lower slopes of the surrounding mountains abounded in game, and, to a certain extent, could be cultivated and used for pasturage in later Neolithic times. At many places around the edge of the plain pile dwellings have been discovered, and there are doubtless countless more Neolithic villages to be revealed. In the case of the Swiss or Italian lake dwellings, where the lakes still exist, excavation can only be carried on at certain seasons of the year when the water is low before spring melts the snow of the higher mountains, or when a long and very hot summer has not only completely melted them but the water therefrom has been drained away. At Loubliana (Laibach), on the other hand, owing to the disappearance of the lake and its replacement by heath conditions, excavation is easy and will in the future yield very important results.

The frontispiece will give a better idea of what one of

these pile-dwelling villages looked like than any amount of description. There must have been a good deal of rude comfort, and seemingly the close proximity to water had no very evil effects. Again, rubbish was readily got rid of by throwing it overboard, probably to the benefit of the health of the inhabitants, but also to the assistance of the modern prehistorian; for in many cases this rubbish and other objects that fell into the water by chance or design have been preserved in the mud and peat at the bottom and can be dug up to-day. Not only do we find pots, stone implements and other objects made of resistant material, but also implements made from antler, as well as seeds of plants, pieces of woven material used for clothes-making and fishing nets and the like.

In our own day there still exist among certain primitive peoples—for example, at Brunei in Borneo—similar lake dwellers, and judging from the remains we have of their Neolithic counterparts, the general life and conditions seem very similar. Even much nearer home we find something of the same sort, although the lake is absent, in the case of granaries and storehouses that are built up on short pillars two or three feet from the ground, their object being to checkmate rats and other vermin that would destroy the store.

The English lake dwellings are all later in date than Neolithic times. The best known, perhaps, are those of Glastonbury which date from the Iron Age; to which era belong most of the so-called crannogs in Ireland, etc.

The building of these lake villages must have necessitated the use of a boat and in exceptional cases the pile dwellings appear to have remained as islands unconnected with the shore so that a boat would be continually needed. No traces of Palaeolithic boats remain, none have been found of Mesolithic date though conditions must often have necessitated the use of simple boats or rafts. In the Metal Ages various forms of boat were common, but only a few Neolithic examples have been found. The simplest type would of course be a scooped-out log with untrimmed ends; such a specimen has been preserved at Lake Bienne. Dr Fox points out that boat-evolution may have proceeded somewhat as follows. After the use of a hollowed log would come the discovery that the pointing of one end was a great advantage while the other would be left square and untouched; finally the builder would find it quicker and easier when hollowing his log to scoop away the whole of this square end and to replace it afterwards with a simple stern-board. Examples of Neolithic boats pointed at one end have been found, and in one or two instances footrests and seats appear.

CAVE HOMES

The use of caves as homes was, of course, perfectly natural, but because in certain parts of the world the Neolithic folk followed the customs of their Palaeolithic forerunners in this respect there is no reason to see any connection between the two civilisations. Obviously caves could only be employed as homes where they occur naturally, that is where the formation of the ground is suitable—practically speaking, only in limestone districts. When excavating Palaeolithic deposits in French or Spanish caves it is very common to find a Neolithic and Early Metal Age layer at the top, and at first sight it might be imagined that the occurrence of Neolithic industries in cave deposits would enable the

prehistorian to use the same stratigraphical methods as
are used for the Palaeolithic cultures and thus obtain a
sequence of succession for the Neolithic civilisation
generally. Unfortunately this has not proved possible;
for one thing, the use of caves for homes by the Neolithic folk was too sporadic, and for another, being close
to the surface and unprotected by layers of stalagmite
(the formation of which was favoured by the changes
of climate in Palaeolithic times) the Neolithic layers
have been the prey of burrowing animals, such as the
rabbit, and little is left of any stratigraphy there may
once have been. It is often common to find Neolithic
and Metal Age layers, all intermixed with mediaeval
material, resting on a layer of stalagmite formed during
the change of climate in Palaeolithic times, which, owing
to its hard compactness, has protected all the older
Palaeolithic industries underneath. At the same time
these cave homes have yielded many Neolithic and
Early Metal Age objects of great interest.

NEOLITHIC ART

Art is such an important index to human thought
and culture that the subject has been treated in a special
chapter. It need only be said here that although the
wondrous Palaeolithic art disappears for ever with the
advent of Mesolithic times, and naturalistic art is extremely rare, pottery is often beautifully engraved with
complicated designs in various techniques; these will be
considered in their proper place. Painting on pots was
practised at the end of the Neolithic and in the beginning
of the Metal Ages in certain definite areas, and the relationships of the different pot-painting cultures is one
of extreme interest. Rock carvings and rock-shelter

paintings occur mostly in the Copper Age, the latter especially in Spain where they form an extremely interesting group.

BURIALS

Burials form a very important branch of study, but these can be dealt with better when the various areas of Neolithic culture are described. They consist for the most part of (1) ordinary graves dug in the ground with little or no indication on the surface, (2) graves with definite mounds, and (3) various megalithic structures sometimes forming tombs of gigantic size. Caves were also sometimes used for the purpose of burial, and interesting examples have been found in North Italy where the bodies, laid straight out, were surrounded with large stones, while close by was buried rich funeral furniture consisting of beautifully made polished tools and other objects. The fact that some of these beautiful tools have been carefully broken in two has given rise to the idea that in some districts Neolithic man had a complicated cult of the dead. Judging from modern analogy these weapons may have been broken so that the spirit of the weapon might accompany the dead man and aid him in the beyond;—it is certainly the case that whatever kind of burial we take, a rich funeral furniture is commonly found. That such a cult should exist is not surprising when we consider that ceremonial burial, involving also the burying of choice weapons, objects of ornament, etc. with the dead had been practised from Middle Palaeolithic times onwards. Death would be one of the first things to strike the imagination of primitive man, and a cult of the dead is after all to be expected as one, at any rate, of the several roots of his religio-emotional development.

AREAS[1] OF CULTURE

If the reader will look back to the section on climate he will see that the Sub-Boreal warm, dry, period did not set in until Mid-Neolithic and the beginning of Early Metal Age times. The warm wet climate prior to this was favourable to forest growth, and it was not everywhere even in western Europe that mankind could penetrate. In England we find Neolithic remains for the most part confined to down lands and the sandy heights overlooking the fens in Norfolk and Suffolk, as well as, of course, along main river valleys. Areas like Huntingdonshire and the clayey midlands were forest areas, and were generally left uninhabited. Again, the greater part of what is to-day Central Germany formed one long stretch of primeval forest, and it is only along its edges or on loess lands unsuitable for forest growth that we should expect to discover rich Neolithic cultures. It was not until the dawn of the Metal Ages was in sight that the increasing dryness caused the forests to dwindle and the great areas that they had occupied to be inhabited. There grew up, therefore, in Europe a certain number of more or less disconnected areas of Neolithic development, which developed independently and only coalesced and bred hybrids when the intervening forest lands became clear. For convenience sake we can take as separate areas the following: an Eastern Area populated by various Asiatic migrations that invaded Eastern Europe firstly by way of the Danube and its tributaries, occupying the loess lands of southern Germany; later via Transylvania. Again, there is a Northern Area that includes Scandinavia and the shores of the Baltic, but which was modified in its development

[1] The word "circle" is sometimes used in place of "area."

not only by influences from the south-west, but also from the east and south-east. Then there is the Western Area, which includes our own country and western Europe generally. The folk of this last area seem to have played a considerable part too, in the development of the later Pile-Dwelling cultures of the highland backbone of the continent. Lastly there is the area of the Mediterranean basin and its shores, where the development was culturally far in advance of that of northern Europe, although it must be allowed that the Spiral Meander pottery of the Eastern Area will stand comparison with even the beautiful ripple ware of Crete.

It must be remembered that the very fact of the community life of Neolithic times, with the specialisation which it engendered, tended to the multiplication of local differences which add enormously to the difficulties of the student, as the industries are far less uniform than was the case in Palaeolithic times.

This division into areas, which were to a great extent separated from each other by forest growth until the end of Neolithic times, must not be taken too strictly. It is convenient to create them for the purposes of study and they have real existence, but at no moment were they completely cut off from one another; and the hybrids produced at the dawn of the Metal Age, when they coalesced in the then forest-free lands, are perfectly bewildering.

RACES(5)

Nothing has been said so far as to the Neolithic race or races. Various criteria have been adopted by the physical anthropologists to differentiate the races of mankind. Thus hair, pigmentation, skull-form, stature, etc., are all employed, and when taken together demonstrate with fair certainty the relationships of any particular people. But taken singly these criteria may be deceptive, just in the same way as typology without the checks of stratigraphy, patina, etc., often leads the student of Palaeolithic times into hopeless error. Only skeletons have survived to help us in determining prehistoric races and these remains—even in the Neolithic and earliest Metal Age Periods—are not very common and often not too well preserved. It follows that it is not always possible to differentiate races with any clearness, and the matter is further complicated in that a school exists which suggests that even such a thing as skull form is partly a resultant of environment, and that a change in latitude or altitude will in time definitely affect the structure of the body(6).

However, the old division of the early inhabitants of Europe into Mediterraneans, Alpines and Nordics, still remains very useful. The Mediterranean race was long-headed, oval-faced and of slender build. This type is found around the Middle Sea and as far north as southern Britain. The same description applies to the Neolithic folk at Anau, which is very important for it is more than possible that the Neolithic civilisation had its cradle in Central Asia. Again, it has been shown that in all probability the old long-headed Capsian folk developed into the Tardenoiseans and, learning something of the new civilisation, became "neolithicised" and formed no small part of the Neolithic stock of the western Mediterranean. Possibly it is better to refer all to a larger race group (Neoanthropic Man) who first arrived in Europe in Upper Palaeolithic times and there underwent considerable modifications. If this be so the men of Anau and of the western Mediterranean would be cousins, as it were, and physically not very dissimilar.

The Alpines were as a whole a very round-headed, broad-faced, thick-set folk, rather taller than the Mediterraneans. They occupied the mountains forming the backbone of Europe and Asia. It used to be thought that it was the round-heads who introduced the Neolithic civilisation into Europe and this theory was strengthened by the finding of a few round-headed skulls associated with the long-headed variety in Mesolithic burials (comp. Ofnet, Mughem, etc.). As it was then an acknowledged fact that no round-heads appeared in Europe before Neolithic times, this seemed conclusive, and it was believed that these Mesolithic round-heads were the forerunners of an invading Neolithic people. The finding of round-headed skulls at Solutré of Upper Palaeolithic (Aurignacian) age has rather modified this conclusion. Again, the earliest Swiss lake culture owes everything to the long-headed Danubians of the Eastern Area, who pushed up the Danube and spread northwards by the Moravian gap into Silesia, and southwards by the Rhine to the Lake of Constance and elsewhere, founding there a culture which only ceased with the rising and overflowing of the lakes, due to climatic changes. The Pile-Dwelling culture later owes more to the Western Area. The Alpines thus were not the first Neolithic folk in the field, at any rate not in western Europe, although further east they no doubt played a greater rôle in very early times.

The cradle of the last or Nordic race is roughly placed in the south of Siberia. This folk seems to have arrived in Europe at a rather later date than the other two unless we are to consider as a proto-Nordic invasion the Upper Palaeolithic Solutreans, who, coming from eastwards, dominated parts of western Europe before vanishing at the rise of the Magdalenians. Burials afford little evidence as they are few and unsatisfactory.

Nordic man was tall and long-headed; some modern Swedes to-day conform closely to the type.

It is interesting to note that trephination of the living human skull was sometimes practised in prehistoric times(7). This fact was noted by Prunières as long ago as 1865. Sometimes a large hole was simply bored; sometimes the same result was obtained by drilling a series of small holes or by scraping out a small circular furrow and then removing the enclosed portion of bone. How this delicate operation could have been performed with only sharp flint tools, and the actuating motive, remain a mystery.

Trephining after the death of the individual is also known, but this was probably merely for convenience in suspending the head, possibly of a dead friend, more probably of some redoubtable foe.

BIBLIOGRAPHY and REFERENCES

(1) H. Gams and R. Nordhagen. *Postglaziale Climaänderungen und erdkrusten Bewegungen in Mitteleuropa,* Munich, 1923.

 C. E. P. Brooks. "The evolution of climate in North-west Europe." *Quart. Journ. Roy. Meteor. Soc.* vol. xlvii, 1921, p. 173.

 —— *The Evolution of Climate,* London, 1922.

(2) T. J. Arne. *Palaeontologia Sinica,* series P, vol. i, fasc. 2. Peking, 1925.

(3) See bibliography (4) at end of chapter ii.

(4) M. de Puydt. A good account will be found in tome xxix, 1910, of the *Mém. Soc. d'Anth. de Bruxelles.* This author has published much on this subject.

(5) A. C. Haddon. *The Races of Man.* 1924.

(6) Sir W. Ridgeway. See *Brit. Ass. (Anth. Sect.),* Dublin, 1908.

(7) T. W. Parry. "The Prehistoric Trephined Skulls of Great Britain, etc." *Proc. Roy. Soc. of Medicine,* vol. xiv, no. 10, Aug. 1921.

 —— "Trephination of the living Human Skull in prehistoric times." *Brit. Med. Journ.* March 1923.

 —— "The collected evidence of Trephination of the Human Skull in Great Britain during prehistoric times." *Proc. Third Internat. Congress of the Hist. of Medicine,* London, July 1922.

TYPOLOGY

I N dealing with Neolithic industries methods similar to those used in describing our Palaeolithic fore-runners can be employed. The various tools can be classed into families, each family containing a number of different types clearly related to one another. Naturally overlap sometimes occurs, and there are cases when it is impossible to say whether a given specimen is the final development of one family or of another. Neolithic man was obviously concerned in making a tool that would do the particular job required, and had little thought or care about conforming exactly to any accurate pattern. From the student's point of view, however, the evolution of these families is very useful, and, to a greater or less extent, they doubtless correspond with the various works which had to be performed by prehistoric man.

CELTS

From a typological point of view the most important family in Neolithic times is undoubtedly the celt. This tool is sometimes made of flint, sometimes of any fine-grained hard rock, whether igneous or sedimentary. As it would seem that a tough edge was required, the latter was mostly used, the former only being requisitioned in areas, like East Anglia, where flint is very common and other hard rocks are almost absent. The tool was made

---

[1] This chapter is largely for reference purposes and describes the various types of tools and pottery; it should be read in conjunction with the succeeding chapters.

either by chipping, or by grinding and polishing, or by a combination of the two techniques. The basal type is the same for both the Northern and Western Areas; celts are not found in the Eastern Area; but from the basal type sprang developments, which are not the same in the north as in the west. The basal type can be seen on reference to Plate 8, nos. 2 and 5. No. 2, from Lakenheath, Suffolk, is made of flint, a chipping technique being alone employed. There is a sharp convex cutting edge, the other or butt end being more or less pointed. In the case of the particular specimen in question a considerable amount of natural crust has been left at the top end, possibly useful as a handhold. The sides are straight and converge towards the butt. No. 5, from Reach Fen, Cambridgeshire, is a ground specimen made of igneous rock. The working edge, as before, is convex, and a section cut through the tool towards the butt end would be circular; which fact is of some importance. Whether these tools were hafted as axes or adzes, or whether they were used as hand tools, it is not easy to say, possibly in both ways. It is not unlikely that in some cases the tool was used as we should use a cold chisel, that is, it was held in position by the hand and the butt end was hammered with a wooden mallet. This would explain the peculiar fractures that are sometimes to be noted at the top end of the tool.

WESTERN AREA

The evolution of the celt in the Western Area is simple to follow. The tool becomes flatter, the section through the butt end from being more or less circular becomes very oval, and in the final development there is little to distinguish the object from a chisel. Plate 8, no. 1, from Burwell Fen, Cambridgeshire, is a good example of a partially polished, partially chipped specimen, with straight, sharp, slightly converging sides running up from the convex working edge to a narrow sharp butt end. No. 4 from Coton, Cambridgeshire, is similar in form though polished throughout. No. 6, as was the case in no. 1, is partly polished, partly chipped, but in this instance the polish is confined solely to the working edge. It comes from Burnt Fen, Cambridgeshire, and is more pointed at the top end than 1 or 4 though the section is very oval. Possibly this is a slightly later characteristic. Varieties, such as Plate 8, no. 3, from Burwell Fen, Cambridgeshire, showing a very definite waist to the tool, are to be considered as chisels, but they cannot logically be separated from a final development of the celt.

NORTHERN AREA

The developments of the celt around the Baltic are not quite the same. If a section through the middle of the basal type be taken, either in the Northern or the Western Area, it will be found to be circular rather than oval; in the first northern development the celt has squared sides and the section becomes an oval, the two ends of which are truncated. This type, which in Scandinavia is found in the dolmens, is figured on Plate 9, no. 4; this specimen, from Sweden, is partly chipped, though mostly polished. As before, the two slightly convergent sides run up from a convex working edge to the butt end, which is not very pointed and is sharp. In the next development the section through the middle of the tool becomes rectangular: many large and beautiful examples of this variety, made solely by chipping, have been found in Danish passage graves.

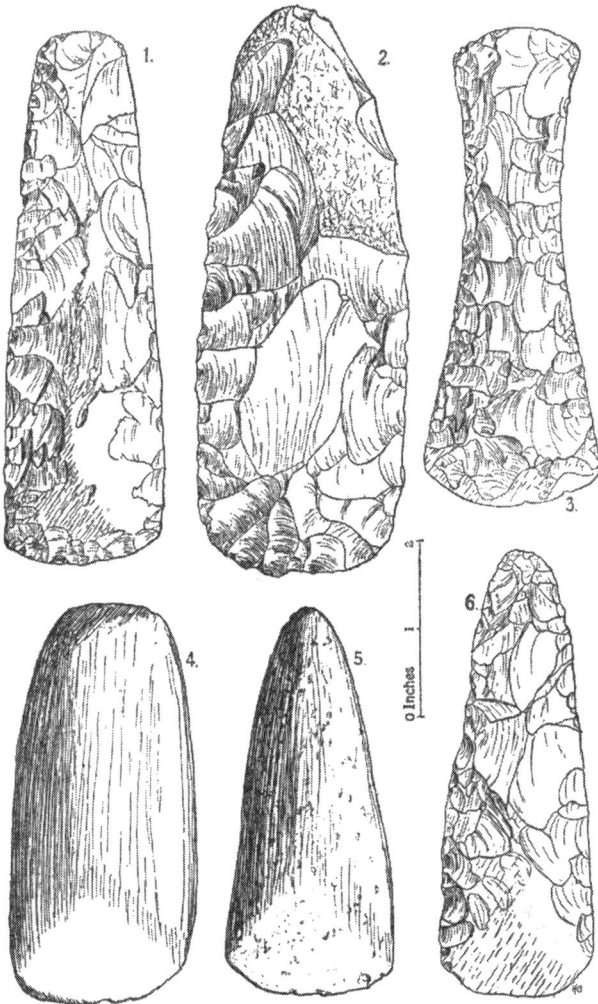

Plate 8. Neolithic tools.

Plate 9, no. 1, from Denmark, is an example made mostly by a chipping technique, though polishing, especially on the side shown in the figure, is not absent. In the final development of the celt the section remains rectangular, but the sides become much more convergent and the butt end more pointed and less sharp. Plate 9, no. 2, is a typical example made of the grey flint so common in Scandinavia; the thick squared sides are boldly blocked out by coarse vertical chipping; a certain amount of polishing is present on the specimen. A small toy example, pierced for suspension, possibly used as an ornament or an amulet, is figured on Plate 12, no. 4; it was found in Aberdeenshire. Many hafted specimens of celts have been found in the Swiss lake dwellings. The haft consists of a piece of antler, the celt being inserted in the hollowed end and held in place by some mastic. Plate 13, no. 7, is a good example, and that such a hafted tool would form a useful hand implement is very evident. No. 6 of the same Plate shows a small celt from the Swiss lakes without its antler haft.

CHISELS, GOUGES, ETC.

It has already been stated that in some cases the final developments of the celt graded into what one would naturally describe as a chisel, but other types exist, as reference to Plate 10, nos. 7 and 8, will at once show. No. 7, from Burwell, Cambridgeshire, is of flint made partly by flaking, partly by polishing. The well-made, working edge is pointed and flattened so as to resemble a screw-driver and is polished on both sides, but the other end, fairly sharp and not very regular, has been mostly chipped; possibly this other end was hafted in a hollow stick. No. 8, from Icklingham, Suffolk, is

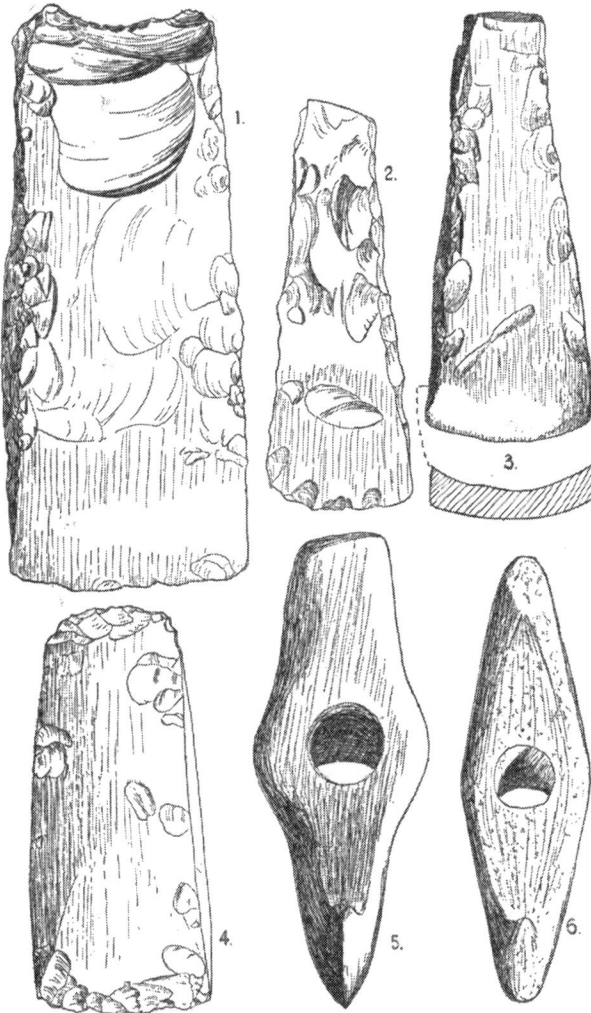

Plate 9. Neolithic tools.

made mostly by chipping; the working edge is regular, differing from the butt end which, though also fairly sharp, is very irregular: it has been damaged in recent times, the patina showing that a modern flake has been removed. Broad chipped chisels, flat on the under-surface and convex on the upper are common at Cissbury. Plate 8, no. 3, a specimen already mentioned in connection with the celts, is very thin compared with its length; the convex working edge shows polishing, though most of the rest of the specimen, including the sharp butt end, is wholly formed by chipping. Plate 11, no. 2, figures a peculiar type of tool from Lakenheath Warren, Suffolk, the exact use of which is unknown. From some points of view it should be classed in the family of the arrow heads, being connected with the transverse-edge variety (see p. 114), the convex sharp edge being the working edge and the lower pointed end being hafted in a stick or bone. Other students have considered, however, that the tool was used as a small convex-edge chisel. Such a shape would be very useful in leather work.

Plate 9, no. 3, illustrates a gouge from Denmark with a section below showing the gouge-like hollow. It is a tool rarely found in Great Britain or the Western Area, but is common in Scandinavia. It is exactly similar to the celt, except that the convex working edge is hollowed out, as in the case of a large modern gouge.

PICKS AND FABRICATORS

A typical pick from Eriswell, Suffolk, is shown on Plate 10, no. 9, and a typical fabricator, from Kentford, Suffolk, on the same plate, no. 11. Implements of the pick type were almost certainly used as cold chisels. They are rough, irregular tools usually made almost

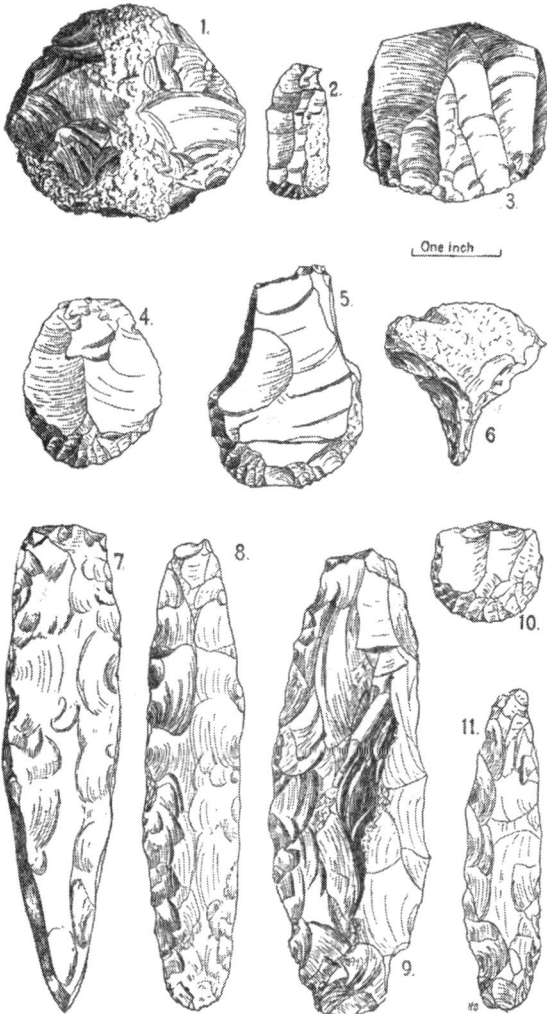

One inch

Plate 10. Neolithic tools.

solely by chipping; and have a fairly narrow sharp end, and a blunt butt end. They were quite suitable for use with a wooden mallet. This tool is very common in Neolithic industries, and with its roughly parallel sides cannot be mistaken for any Palaeolithic forerunner. Examples ten inches or more in length have been found.

The fabricator is a much smaller tool, often blunt at both ends. The student might perhaps regard it as a stone finger, and it was probably used for the thousand and one purposes in which a live finger would get damaged. Doubtless, too, it was used as a small punch.

SCRAPERS

Scrapers of all varieties and shapes abound in Neolithic industries. Examples can be seen on Plate 10, nos. 2, 3, 4, 5 and 10. The first of these, which is a Belgian example of Omalian date, shows a typical end-scraper on a short blade. No. 3, from Icklingham, Suffolk, is a core-scraper—sometimes called a "tea-cosy," being in shape not unlike one of these articles. Nos. 4 and 5 are made on flakes, no. 4 comes from near Grimes Graves and no. 5 from Eastbourne. Slight differences can be noted; for example, no. 4 has a low keel running up the flake which is completely absent from no. 5. In the case of these four examples the working edge was obtained by chipping, percussion being used. In the case of no. 10, from Icklingham, Suffolk, however, pressure flaking has been employed; the flake scars show a scaling as if fragments of flint like fish scales had been removed; the facets are covered with fine ripple marks, giving to the whole a rather glassy or waxy appearance[1]. This latter appearance, due to pressure flaking, is in all probability a sign that the

[1] This is not seen when the object is patinated.

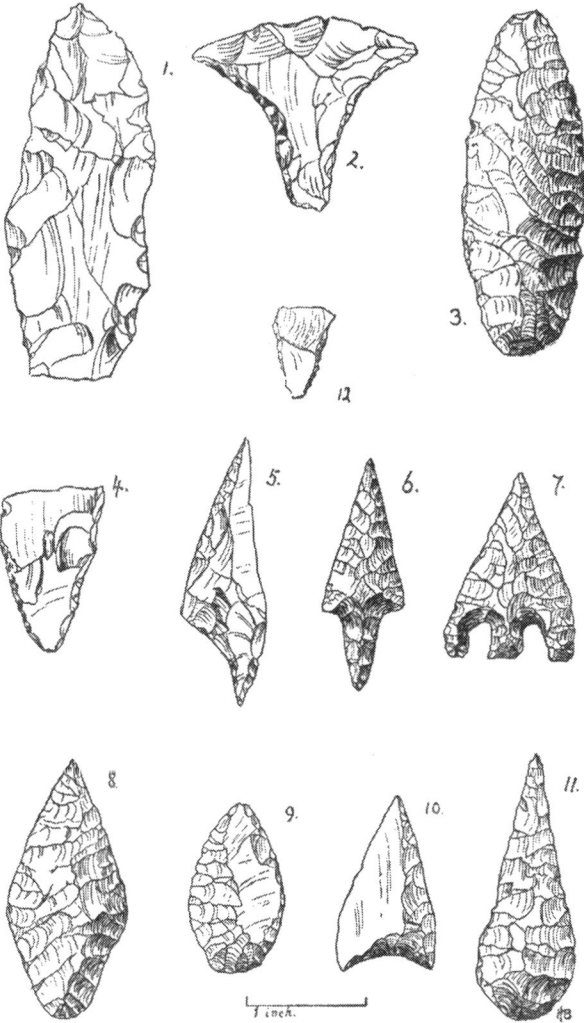

Plate 11. Neolithic and Earliest Metal Age tools,

tool can be regarded as being of the Early Metal Age. Similar tools have been found with burials in the Beaker Age.

SLUGS

Another tool on which this glassy or waxy appearance is common is the so-called slug—Plate 11, no. 3. This tool is made on a blade, the under surface being the flake surface; the upper surface is convex, trimmed all over by pressure flaking. Where this top surface is very convex and the flint is unpatinated, the appearance, at first sight, is not unlike those repulsive slugs found in damp bogs. However, in many cases the top surface is not so convex, and in some instances, where the specimens are patinated, the name no longer applies. The use of these tools is unknown.

SICKLES

Some form of sickle is essential to the agriculturist and examples of such a tool are not infrequent. They usually consist of several medium-sized stout flakes with sharp, often denticulated edges, hafted in some such fashion as indicated in Plate 12, no. 5. If the working edge of a sickle is turned to the light, it will be seen, except in cases that have been subsequently heavily patinated, that the action of the straw on the flint has produced a veritable polishing at the extreme edge, with an appearance comparable to that of sand polishing in the desert. This is a very good test as to whether a not particularly denticulated blade has been utilised as a sickle. Naturally it is quite impossible to give this appearance in a pen and ink drawing. Plate 12, nos. 2 and 6, are examples of sickle tools, the former from Scandinavia, the latter an African specimen from the Siwa Oasis.

DAGGERS

Metal appeared early in the south of Europe and much later in the north, but certain stray metal tools were introduced, doubtless by commerce, which were copied in stone. The result, as seen in Plate 12, no. 1, is a splendid dagger, the blade being beautifully trimmed and very thin when compared with its length. The handle is much stouter, and in many specimens is decorated by a small row of tubercles along its length, doubtless to ensure a good handgrip. The specimen figured is from Scandinavia where metal was particularly late in being introduced. Plate 12, no. 3, is an example of a different type, from Belgium; the material is Grand Pressigny flint introduced by commerce, and the lower third has its edges carefully blunted to ensure a satisfactory grip, the upper two-thirds being chipped sharp to make the object into a satisfactory weapon. These daggers are late in age and possibly should be considered as belonging to the dawn of the Metal Ages, even though metal itself was not yet in full use in the regions where they are found.

ARROW HEADS

The family of the arrow heads is large and complicated. One type is figured in Plate 11, no. 7, from Burnt Fen, Cambridgeshire, and shows a more or less thin triangular piece of flint chipped all over, having a stout central tang, into which the backbone of the flint runs, and two side wings. These wings doubtless functioned as barbs. Sometimes the barbs are very divergent: sometimes, as in the example figured, they curve round so that they run almost parallel to one another. The former type is thought to be slightly earlier than the one illustrated. Plate 11, no. 10, from Eriswell, Suffolk, shows a variety having two wings but no tang, this type is generally called a hollow-base arrow head. In Plate 11, no. 6, however, we note the tang without the wings. These arrow heads begin in definitely Neolithic times, although fairly late on in the period, but they continue well into Metal Age times. Plate 11, no. 5, from Fordham, Cambridgeshire, is an example of a barbed point. From some points of view it might be considered as a single-winged example to be hafted, like the other arrow heads, on the end of a stick; but in all probability it is more of the nature of a large harpoon barb, the shorter edge being let into a groove on the side of a pointed stick or bone and held in place by some mastic, a method similar to that described in connection with Maglemosean culture. The point (*a*) would then form the barb of the tool: both right and left handed barbed points have been found. Plate 11, no. 4, from Undley, Suffolk, is a large example of what is known as a transverse arrow head and no. 12 is a typical example from Belgium; unlike the other varieties it is an early type and is found in Mesolithic times. The business end instead of being a point is a cutting edge, the sides being squared and the butt roughly pointed. A clear connection with Plate 11, no. 2, has already been mentioned. Plate 11, no. 1, from Icklingham, Suffolk, is a good example of a small leaf-shaped javelin head. These tools are very similar to the Solutrean laurel leaves of Upper Palaeolithic date, being chipped on both the upper and the lower surfaces. They are often of great size; and these large, thin, beautifully made tools have been found in burials associated with the first appearance of metal. Small, thin-as-paper, leaf-shaped arrow heads are known; these being also in most cases of

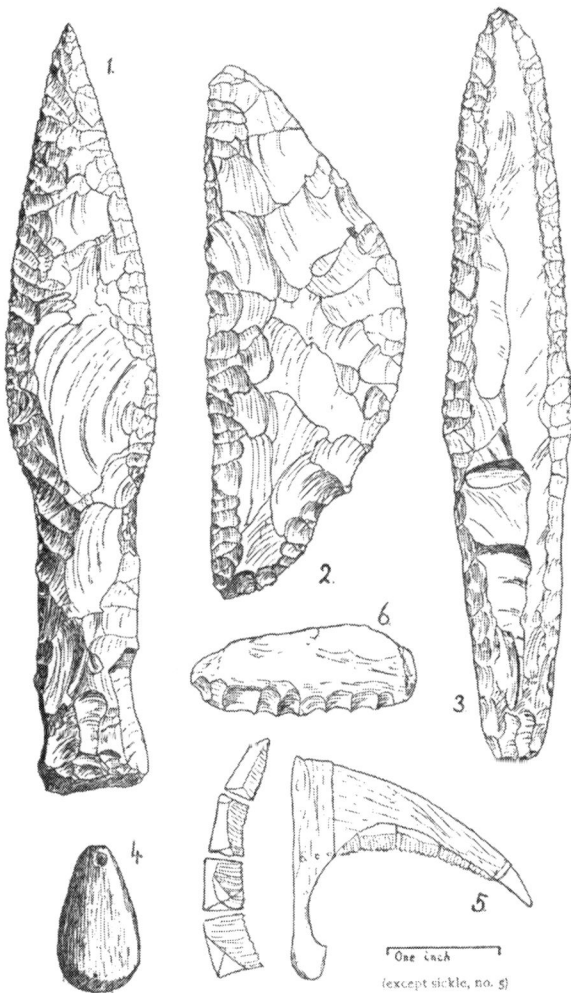

Plate 12. Neolithic and Earliest Metal Age tools.

One inch
(except sickle, no. 5)

Early Metal Age date. Plate 11, no. 9, from Burnt
Fen, Cambridgeshire, is a good example. On account
of its oval shape this variety has sometimes been called
a lozenge. Plate 11, no. 11, from Quy, Cambridgeshire,
shows a long, very pointed and particularly thin specimen, and Plate 11, no. 8, depicts a variety from Brandon,
Suffolk, which has "hips" a third of the way up on
either side, in some specimens these are even more
marked. This angularity undoubtedly indicates a late
age.

AWLS

Two kinds of awl exist: the real awl and the pseudo-
awl. In the real awl the working point is chipped all
round, so that its section would be roughly circular.
In the pseudo-awl the whole is made on a flake, and
the flake surface continues right up to the point; the
section instead of being circular is therefore ∩-shaped.
The latter is by far the commoner, although it would
seem to be more liable to break and less efficient for
use. Plate 10, no. 6, is an example of an awl, the butt
end on the upper surface being largely covered by
natural crust. These tools were no doubt constantly
required for piercing holes in skins and for many other
purposes.

HAMMER AXES AND SHOE-LAST
SHAPED TOOLS

There are two tools typical of the Eastern Area: one
is the hammer axe and the other is the so-called shoe-
last shaped tool; the former is figured in Plate 13, no. 1,
the latter on the same plate, no. 2 and on Plate 21, no. 15.
The hammer axe, as its name implies, has an axe edge
at one end, the other being heavy and blunt, so that it

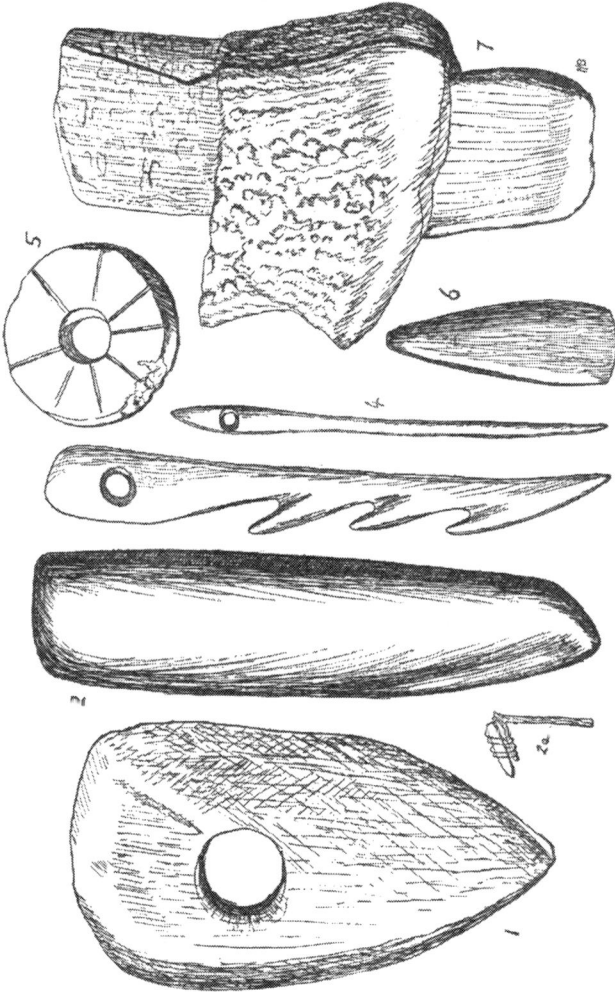

Plate 13. Neolithic tools.

could be used as a hammer; in fact the object resembled a household chopper. It is pierced with a hole for hafting purposes, the direction of the hole showing that an axe not an adze was required. These tools are often not particularly well made, nor are the sides particularly regular; though they are generally ground. The shoe-last tool, on the other hand, made of fine-grained igneous rock is often beautifully made and polished; it shows a flat under surface, the upper surface being highly convex. One end is blunt; at the other, the convex upper surface curves round to join the flat under surface which rises slightly to meet it. The imple-ment was certainly an agricultural tool, possibly used as the share of a plough, as discussed in a previous chapter, or it may have been hafted on to a forked piece of wood, as in Plate 13, no. 2a, and used as a hoe; it may also sometimes have been used as a cold chisel. The type is not found in the west.

BATTLE AXES

Battle axes are a large and complicated family and were made by a folk who, possibly cradled in South Russia, invaded the Northern Area fairly early on in Neolithic times, and there developed. As a warrior people they spread far and wide, dominating large tracts of Europe and forming hybrids with other peoples. Plate 9, no. 5, shows a late example, prob-ably dating from the period when the northern influence had penetrated right down to Switzerland, and illus-trates the characteristic form, blunt at one end, with a sharp working edge turned up like the prow of a boat, the whole being pierced for hafting. Plate 9, no. 6, shows an example from Denmark, almost certainly from Jutland, of a late development called the canoe-shaped or boat-shaped axe, where both ends are turned up and the whole has been likened, perhaps fancifully, to a Canadian canoe. Many other examples are known, various districts providing special varieties. A few of these can be seen on Plate 14. Battle axes were always pierced for hafting.

VARIOUS

Plate 13, nos. 3 and 4, are examples of a bone harpoon and a rough bone needle from Switzerland. Bone needles or awls (the former being eyed, the latter not) are fairly common in Neolithic industries, but the bone harpoon is more or less confined to Switzerland. The base is pierced with a round hole for suspension; the tool is sometimes single and sometimes double-barbed; the material is stag's horn, and the technique of the barbs, especially in the rough stag's horn varieties, is such that no student who has once seen examples would mix these Neolithic harpoons with either Palaeolithic or Mesolithic specimens. Plate 13, no. 5, is a stone whorl from Scotland, decorated with lines radiating from the central hole. These whorls, which are often made of terra cotta, are common in Neolithic industries and were probably used for a variety of purposes where a weight was required: in weaving, for example, or perhaps, in the case of rough specimens, as sinkers for fishing nets, etc. There is little to remark about them; they vary in size to a certain extent, and are found from Neolithic to quite late times. Plate 14, no. 1, is an example of a pierced hammer stone, the hole being splayed both above and below. This is a Neolithic characteristic, and it was not till Early Metal Age times that primitive man was able to drill a cylindrical hole through stone. Plate 10, no. 1, is an ordinary hammer stone, formed from a lump of flint and found at Brandon, Suffolk. Where possible, a tougher material was preferred, as flint is inclined to shatter easily. It is not always easy to tell when one of these round, spherical objects has really been used as a hammer stone, for when made of hard material they do not bruise easily. Plate 14, no. 2, has been described as a hollow scraper. It is a type common in the north of Ireland but very rare elsewhere, although an example has been found at Cambridge; it has been suggested that the tool was used for rubbing down small wooden shafts, but it would seem to be almost too fragile for this purpose. The hollow is formed by fine, careful, regular chipping. The specimen figured comes from Ballymena, Antrim. Plate 14, no. 3, is another Antrim type which does not seem to occur elsewhere. It consists of a roughly pointed blade or flake, there being little or no secondary working. The under surface is a flake surface showing a good bulb of percussion but without a prepared striking platform. The base, however, has been formed by careful chipping into a definite, though coarse tang, and the whole would seem to have been used as a rough arrow or javelin point. The nearest analogous type is seen on Plate 14, no. 4, an example from Denmark, which also shows a single, carefully made tang; but in this case the specimen shows a lot of secondary working, and although thick and coarse, can only be distinguished from the one shown in Plate 11, no. 6, which has already been described, by the fact that it is not chipped all round; but the under surface, as in the case of the last-mentioned Antrim specimen, is a flake surface. Examples have been found in East Anglia, e.g. at Rushford. The Danish example, however, is probably very late in date, whereas the Antrim tool would appear to belong to an earlier Neolithic Age. Round and squared discs

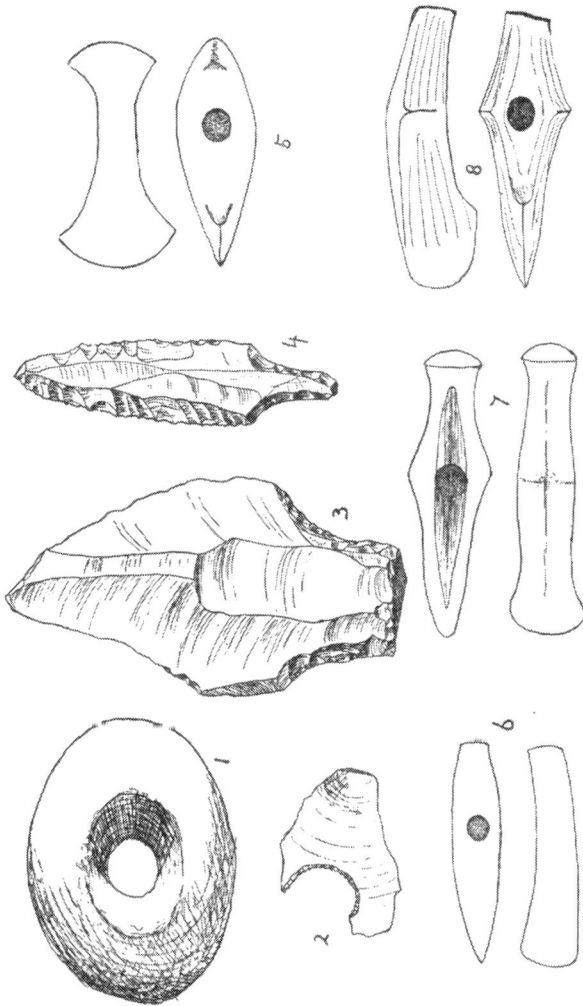

Plate 14. Neolithic tools.

occur in Neolithic industries; the latter are sometimes called skinning knives. The tool is chipped all over on its upper and lower surfaces and the circumference forms a sharp cutting edge. Large cores are also fairly common; from large examples found at Grand Pressigny and called "pounds of butter" very long, regular blades were obtained.

POTTERY

Types of pots, as well as their decoration, vary so much in different localities that only a generalised description, giving certain well-defined types, is here possible. Plate 15, nos. 1–4, illustrate the pottery and decoration typical of the Spiral-Meander culture of the Eastern Area. Note in no. 3 how, twice, the line of the Meander ends in a small depression. In some cases these depressions become more numerous and the Meanders more angular and the resulting decoration has been likened to the large notes in old cathedral psalter books and called *Notenschrift*. Note also nos. 1 and 4 where the small lugs are pierced with vertical holes, for suspending the pot in a sort of net. Nos. 6 and 8 illustrate decorated pots of the so-called Hinkelstein ceramic, another Eastern Area pottery group; nos. 5, 7, 13 are the South German Rössen types which are yet another variant, and perhaps rather later in date. No. 9 is a typical example of *Stichband* where the lines are no longer engraved but consist of punctuations. This technique was developed at the end of Spiral-Meander pottery times in the Danube area. Note that the decoration has become much more angular; the Meanders have become zigzags. Much punctuation decoration occurs at the end of Danubian I times and the sherds nos. 10, 11 and 12 are interesting in this connection.

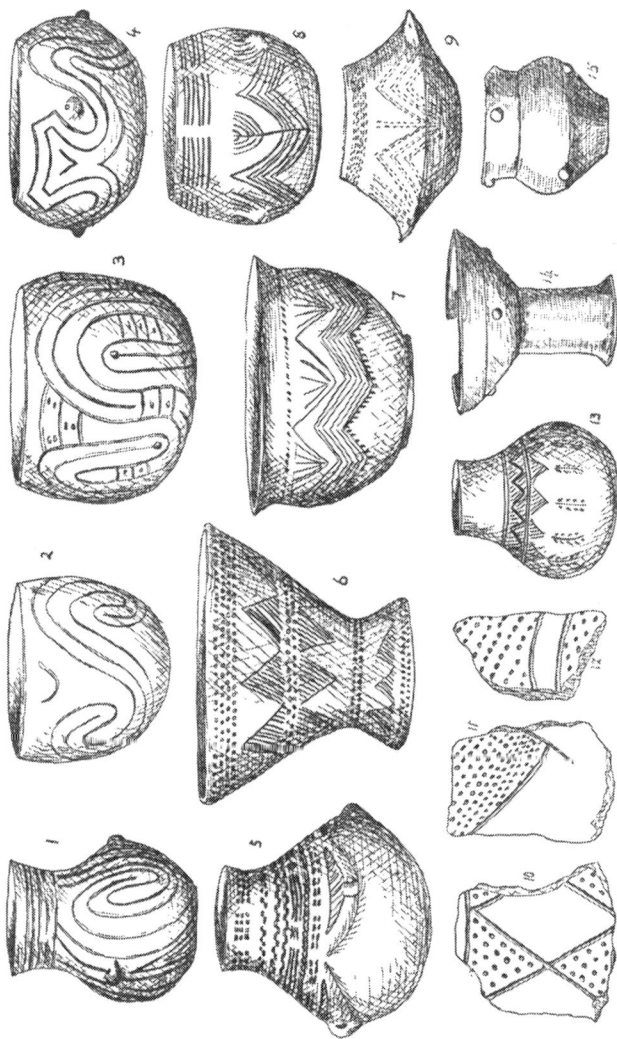

Plate 15. Examples of decorated Neolithic pottery belonging to the culture of the Eastern Area.

No. 10 comes from the Danube valley, nos. 11 and 12 from the Omalian industry of Belgium. Already before the Danubian II period the eastern culture was influencing the western. Nos. 14 and 15 are types typical of Danubian II. The first is a footed vessel and should be compared with Plate 17, no. 4, from the Northern Area. However, the great quantity of these footed vessels found in Hungary and Bavaria as early as Danubian II times precludes the likelihood of their having been derived from a northern type. Note the small button-like protuberances on these Danubian II pots. By Danubian III times the "mixed" cultures had already begun and influences from elsewhere were affecting the Eastern Area.

Plate 16 illustrates types from the Western Area and Pile-Dwelling cultures. No. 1 is a "tulip pot" and nos. 4, 5, 6, 7, 11, 12 represent types of pots and decoration motifs from the French fortified village site of Camp de Chassey. No. 8 is a portion of a Pile-Dwelling cup showing the typical handle. Nos. 3 and 10 are also examples from the pile dwellings and show the typical finger print decoration just by the rim. No. 9 is an example from Mortlake on the Thames and is beautifully decorated.

The pottery of the Northern Area is represented on Plate 17. Nos. 7 and 11 are examples of the "Comb" pottery made by a little known folk who apparently invaded the Baltic area early in Neolithic times. Nos. 3, 6 and 1—the collar flask, the round amphora and the high-necked round amphora—are the most typical examples of the Northern Area culture. No. 10 is a derivative of the round amphora which was found in Germany and no. 5 is a double-conical hanging pot typical of later Passage Grave times in Denmark. The close,

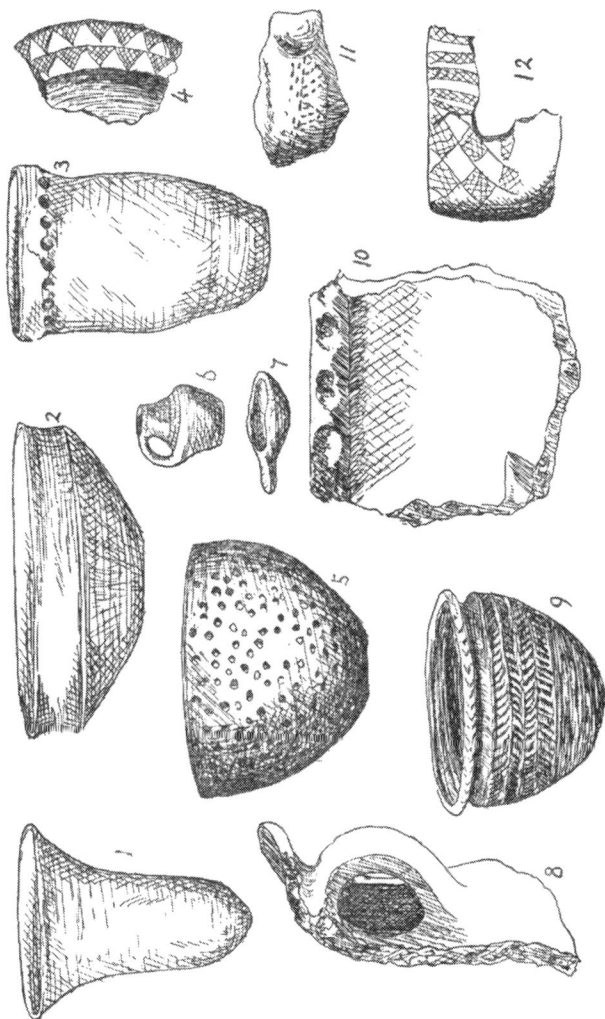

Plate 16. Examples of Neolithic pottery belonging to the culture of the Western Area.

deep zigzag decoration, as seen on nos. 2 and 9 is also specially typical of the northern cultures. As a general rule the northern pottery gives the impression of great vigour but some ruggedness; the fine delicate work we find in the Eastern Area is absent. The results, however, show a high degree of artistic skill.

Plate 18 gives some examples of the so-called "Mixed" cultures due to the coalescing of the cultures of the various areas when the primaeval forests disappeared on the change of climate at the end of Neolithic times. Naturally the influence of different cultures predominates in different localities and it would be instructive for the student to determine which dominates in any given instance on Plate 18. Thus nos. 1 and 9 are clearly Pile-Dwelling types. No. 10 shows the close zigzag of the Northern Area. No. 6 is an example of the corded ware, the decoration being obtained by impressing the paste before firing with a twisted string or cord. This culture is clearly allied with that of the north, as the round amphora (no. 4) is found in it. No. 5 is an example of a late development of the corded ware. Nos. 7, 8 and 9 come from Aichbühl on the Federsee and clearly owe most to the Pile-Dwelling culture; nos. 1 and 2 from Michelberg also show the western influence.

Plate 19 shows some typical beakers, mostly English specimens. These have been divided by Abercromby into three groups: (1) high-brimmed globose cups, (2) ovoid cups with low curved brims, (3) low-brimmed cups. The first of these, shown by Plate 19, no. 2, is a common type in South Britain; the body of the beaker is more or less globular and separated by a constriction from the upper portion, which spreads out like a flower, often equalling the body in height and forming the rim,

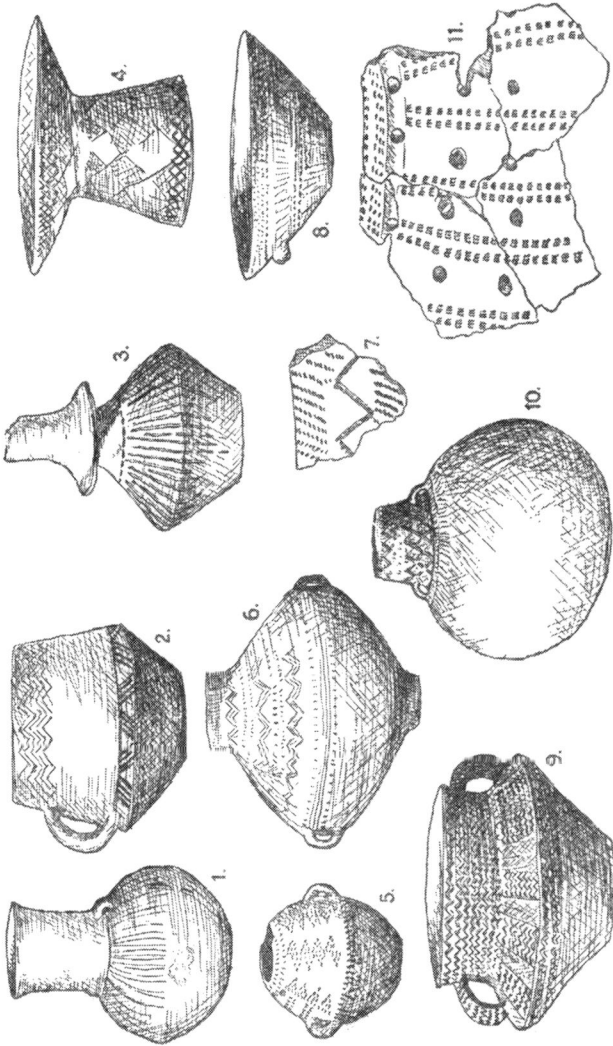

Plate 17. Examples of decorated Neolithic pottery belonging to the culture of the Northern Area.

rising perhaps obliquely but not recurved. In the second type there is no distinct division between the body and the rim, and the rim is strongly curved outwards at the lip (Plate 19, nos. 1 and 5). The main body of the pot is globular rather than oval. The material used for making the pots was extremely carefully chosen and the pots are generally thinner than those of the first variety. They were often fired in presence of air and so had a red colour. Type 3, which is especially common in the north of England and Scotland, is considered by Abercromby to be only a debased variety of type 1; the body is oval rather than globular, but the brim is much lower and is only a fraction of the length of the body (Plate 19, no. 3). Foreign examples show many varieties (Plate 19, no. 4). In some cases the vessel rests on little legs (Plate 19, no. 6). Mugs with handles are also found, and these latter were introduced later into England, where a few examples occur (Plate 19, no. 7) [1].

[1] Note that the decoration motifs are not confined to the particular type of beaker on which they are shown in the plate.

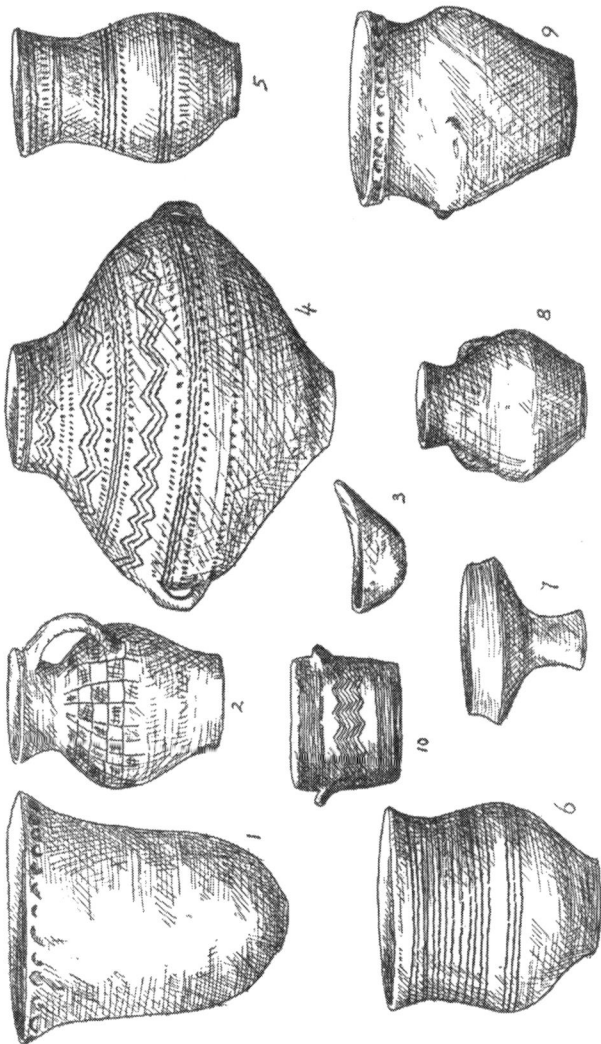

Plate 18. Examples showing types of "mixed culture" pottery that developed in Late Neolithic times in Central Europe.

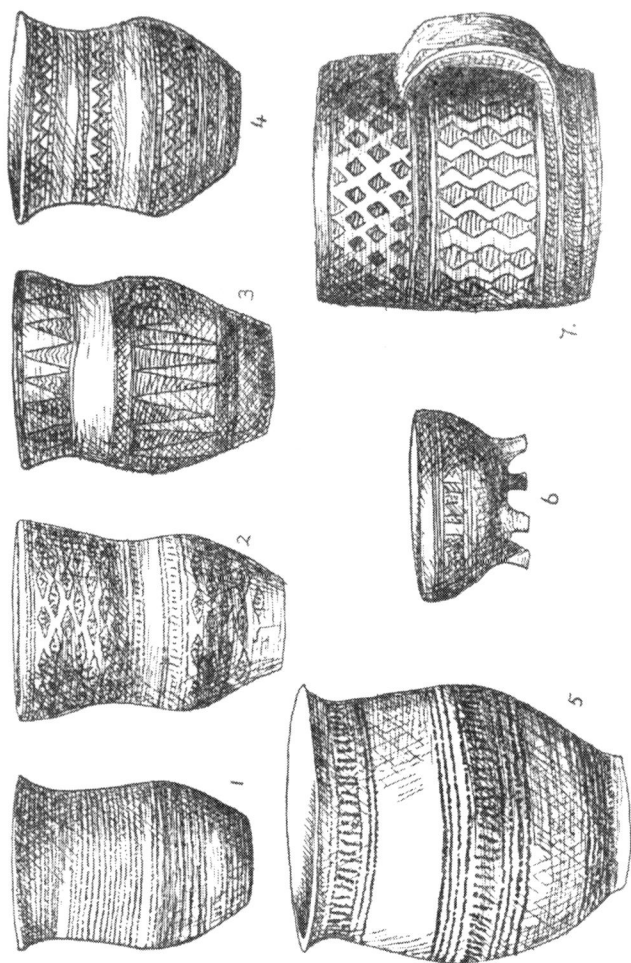

Plate 19. Examples showing types of the Beaker pottery of the Copper Age.

CHAPTER V

NEOLITHIC CULTURES OF THE EASTERN AREA AND LATE NEOLITHIC TIMES IN CENTRAL EUROPE

CENTRAL Asia with its present desert wastes, where formerly, under different climatic conditions, broad pasture lands doubtless extended, was probably the cradle of our Neolithic civilisation and of many of our domestic animals. So we should naturally expect to find that a Neolithic culture would early be flourishing in eastern Europe and are not therefore surprised to find in the earliest Neolithic period around the basin of the Danube peoples practising agriculture and the domestication of animals, apparently unwarlike and leading a simple peasant existence[1]. They were expert in pottery making, being very careful in the choosing of the raw material, with the result that their pots are a joy to behold and handle. The pots are as a rule of a greyish colour, being made from beautifully smoothed paste and often finely decorated. The usual shape is that of a cup or basin with rounded bottom, and a certain amount of neck is sometimes added. There is nothing in the way of a true handle, though two or more lugs are often attached around the pot about two thirds up from the base. The lugs themselves are little conical projections sometimes pierced with a small vertical hole, though larger varieties, pointed and rather like the horn at the ends of a long-bow, are not unknown[2]. The holes are usually quite small in diameter, and it seems probable that these pots with their rounded bottoms were carried in small hammock-like nets, the ends of which were passed through the holes. The decoration in early times was exclusively by engraving and consisted of a series of spiral-like curved lines or zigzags. A favourite motif consists of large zigzag lines, small depressions occurring where the lines meet; the general appearance is a little like early manuscript music and has been named, therefore, rather fancifully, *Noten-schrift* decoration. Two stone agricultural weapons are common: one known as the shoe-last chisel or hoe and the other the hammer axe [1]. Small chipped flint and obsidian flakes and knife blades occur, both the coloured and the black variety of the latter material being very common in Hungary, although examples have also been found in Lower Austria and elsewhere. Some of these little chipped flint tools almost recall the so-called Tardenoisean types, although there is no reason to suspect any connection between the cultures. The people lived in villages, the houses being usually small and oval in shape, and generally slightly excavated in the manner of the Belgian *fonds de cabanes* of the Hesbaye which they closely resemble and which have been already described. The food pit is generally found inside or close to a hut, sometimes one pit may have served several houses. These villages grew up in suitable localities; a good supply of fresh water being, of course, a *sine qua non*.

Little is known about the people themselves as hardly any of their graves have been preserved. They would seem however to have been a tall long-headed folk. Apparently the dead were buried in flat graves without mound or tumulus, the body being flexed. Although inhumation was the almost universal rule

[1] For description of these see the chapter on Typology.

both in Periods Danubian I and Danubian II, isolated cases of cremation have been observed.

Although the cultures of this Eastern Area are called Danubian, it must be noted that their distribution was far wider than the valley of the Danube. In different districts local names have been given and the cultures to which they refer are of course not all precisely similar. Thus in the Danube regions the earliest culture is named, from the typical decoration on the pottery, Spiral-Meander; elsewhere there is the Hinkelstein culture of Württemberg, Baden, Bavaria, Hesse, and as far west as Alsace, and the South German Rössen culture which as a whole is perhaps rather later in date judging from the fact that certain influences from the true Rössen people living to the north can be traced in the pottery. But differences in time as well as area exist and a sequence of at least three periods has been determined. These are due partly to an evolution *in situ*, partly to the action of outside influences. The latter were particularly strong in the last (Danubian III) period when the influence of the Northern Area became especially marked owing to the partial disappearance of the great primaeval forests of Central Germany.

It is convenient to treat Moravia as the typical area as many examples of the splendid pottery already described have been found there. At first the decoration consists usually of curves and meanders and is firm and clear (Plate 15, nos. 1–4). Later the pots still remained simple in form, but the plain spiral-meander and *Notenschrift* decoration in single engraved lines was replaced by a technique of fine punctuated lines known as *Stichband*. The whole appearance of the decoration became more angular, the meanders becoming straight and the wide zigzags long and narrow, their angles acute instead of obtuse. New decoration motifs also appear. This development of Danubian I, like the true Spiral-Meander culture, spread up the Danube and its tributaries as well as northwards through Moravia(3). The earliest industries of the Swiss lake dwellings owe practically everything to the Danubian culture. The whole of Central Germany was still covered by forests and therefore as yet uninhabited, but, following the forest-free loess lands, this eastern European peasant folk actually seem to have penetrated as far west as Belgium where a Neolithic industry called Omalian certainly contains examples of its pottery with the punctuation decoration motifs (Plate 15, nos. 10, 11, 12—the first is an eastern European sherd, the two latter from Belgium). Southwards the Danubian culture came in contact with the far more developed and brilliant cultures of the Mediterranean basin, where metal was not unknown. Considerable intercourse between the two regions can be traced by a study of the respective industries.

The Danubian II culture which followed is largely an evolution of the older culture; but in Hungary (for example at the well-known site at Lengyel(4)) and in Bavaria it is especially characterised by the occurrence of large numbers of footed vessels (Plate 15, no. 14) and pots ornamented with little round knobs (Plate 15, no. 15). Numbers of socketed ladles also occur. Human figurines had already been made by the first Danubian folk, but in second Danubian times they show great skill in manufacture—a seated figure carrying a baby, from the second level at Vinča(5), a site near Belgrade, is really delightful[1].

[1] The earliest level at Vinča can be correlated with Danubian I of Moravia. V. G. Childe believes that the Danubians arrived in Europe by the Danube, Vinča I being, therefore, especially early.

By the next period (Danubian III) the change of climate at the end of Neolithic times had already begun to operate and the forests of the central lands were gradually disappearing. Influences from the north begin to appear and at the same time the Pile-Dwelling culture of the highland region to the south began to spread beyond its borders. The result was that the peasant population of the loess plains became affected by these northern and southern influences, the intensity of each varying naturally with the particular locality. In such an area as Lower Austria the Pile-Dwelling influence is the stronger, and we find handled cups of coarse though well-burnt pottery, typical of the Pile-Dwelling industries; but little influence from the north is apparent, except the occasional occurrence of a few potsherds engraved with deep lines forming close zigzags, which strongly recall northern types.

A little later when the central districts of Germany were forest-free and definitely inhabited, hybrids developed between the cultures of the various areas and these in their turn influenced and sometimes dominated the old peasant stock which we have been describing and who, engaged as they were in agriculture, never seem to have developed the warlike arts.

But this brings us to the whole question of the Late Neolithic cultures in Central Europe formed by the intermixture of the old stocks. The matter is extraordinarily complicated and only a brief sketch is here possible. In Thuringia there developed a culture characterised by its methods of pottery decoration. Before being burnt the paste was impressed with a twisted cord or string and its makers are therefore known as the Corded Ware folk. These people were hardy and warlike, owing as they did a great deal to the northern stock from which they largely sprang. They possessed the battle axe, and their northern relationship is further seen by the presence of the round amphora. They were a long-headed people who interred their dead, in either a squatting or an extended position, in small stone kists or in shallow pit graves covered with a low mound. A rich funeral furniture including pottery, battle axes, hammer axes, pierced teeth, and the like, is often found. Cremation was very rarely practised. A careful study of the Corded Ware culture has enabled investigators to determine an older and a later series showing considerable development in the interval. These were some of the folk who lived side by side with and dominated the old peasant Danubians; it is the Corded Ware people who inhabited the hills, living in fortified localities, while the Danubians lived in unprotected villages in the valleys below.

The so-called Rössen culture(a), whose cradle seems to have been near Merseburg, is another hybrid which owes much to the Northern Area folk. As before, the round amphora occurs as well as round and flat-bottomed bowls which are profusely and beautifully decorated with small complicated geometric patterns. On the other hand, especially in South Germany, the hammer axe and shoe-last shaped chisel or hoe (Plate 11, no. 2) are found together with ceramic forms which demonstrate that the Danubian culture of the Eastern Area also entered largely into the admixture. The cemeteries near Merseburg show inhumation in small kists under barrows, the body being flexed, but cremation was practised at a rather later date. The Rössen folk spread to the regions of the Elbe, Saale and central and southwestern Germany, where, like their Corded Ware relations, they formed a warrior race. The houses, as seen at the village site of Grossgartach in Württemberg, were usually square or rectangular, and were often on two levels. Below was the kitchen and hearth, with a refuse pit near the exit, above were the sleeping quarters. As usual in Neolithic times the walls were constructed of wooden joists interfilled with wicker work daubed over with clay.

Towards the south the influence of the Pile-Dwelling folk was more strongly felt, and there arose a series of cultures that were all closely interrelated. They have been classed together as the Aichbühl mixed culture, from the finds at Aichbühl in Württemberg(a). The admixture was doubtless of hybrids like the Corded Ware folk, etc.; not of the pure races of the several areas. The decoration motifs on the pottery show strong influence both from the north and from the pile-dwellings; thus we note the fine deep lozenge and zigzags recalling Scandinavia, and the small round pits around the rims typical of the Lake-Dwellings pottery. But though a general name has been adopted to denote these Late Neolithic mixed cultures of the south, they are by no means all alike and the pottery of Aichbühl is by no means exactly similar to its contemporary of the Mondsee nor to that found at Loubliana (Laibach) (Plate 20).

Lastly the Beaker folk, cradled in Spain, arrived to add their quota to the welter of peoples that had by now grown up in Central Europe. Their typical vessel was the beaker described in chapter IV, and archers' wrist guards made of stone are common. They already knew of the use of copper for the purposes of tool-making. Their dead were generally interred though two instances of cremation have been found in Moravia. How they reached Central Europe and spread as far east as Silesia and Hungary is not quite clear. The natural route would be via France and the Belfort gap, but it is just here that finds are rarest. However, Beaker folk were at this time in the north of Italy, and it is possible that the warm dry climate had by now opened the Brenner Pass, which a little later, in Bronze Age times, became such an important commercial route.

In Late Neolithic times a new folk appear in eastern Europe, who made a well-burnt, beautifully painted pottery. Stratigraphically two periods have been determined, but as yet little is known about them; did they originate in South Russia or further eastwards? An acquaintance with the use of copper, especially in the later period, is certain.

It appears that these people were already inhabiting fortified villages in Transylvania in Late Danubian II times for, at a site called Erösd numbers of the footed vessels typical of the Danubian II culture have been found together with their painted pottery. Were these people in Transylvania and the lands to the eastward at a still earlier date? Was it they who forced the Battle-Axe folk to go northwards towards the Baltic when they left South Russia to trek westwards? Although the painted pottery culture did not spread to any very great extent, it has been recognised in a number of localities from the south of Russia to Thessaly. The more important sites are, Tripolje, 40 miles south of Kief; Petreny, in Bessarabia; Erösd, in Transylvania, the industry at which last place can be correlated with that found in the lower levels at the next site Cucuteni, in Moldavia, where two distinct levels are found. Several sites are known in Galicia. In the Bukowina Schipenitz(6), one of the type stations of this painted ware culture has been excavated. The typical

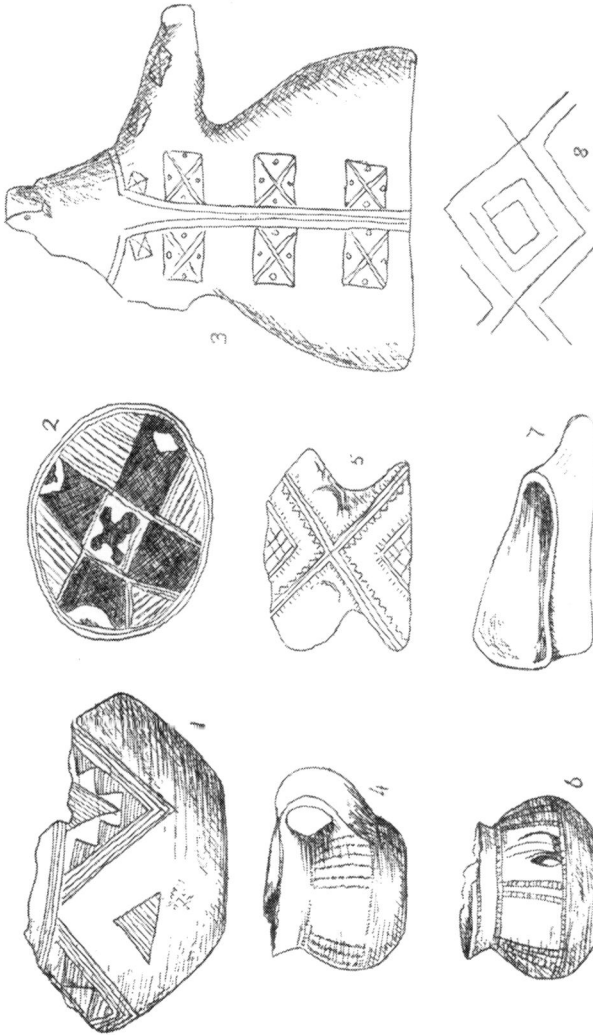

Plate 20. Laibach pottery: Forms and designs drawn from rough sketches made in the Museum at Loubliana (Laibach).

Schipenitz pottery was carefully burnt throughout, even in the case of thick specimens. A reddish coloured, well-washed and carefully selected clay has been used. The colours employed include deep red, yellow, and brown and creamy white: they are sometimes applied direct to the polished surface, sometimes a slip is employed.

The occurrence of this painted ware in Thessaly(7) is important and in that region four cultural periods have been recognised. The pottery of Period I was beautifully made and decorated with well painted geometric patterns, red and white as well as brown paint having been employed. There was also some incised ware with a punctuation technique and a fine, thin, grey, undecorated ware not unlike some Neolithic pottery found in the Peloponnese. It is not yet known whence this culture arrived in Thessaly or what its relationships are, the occurrence of some shoe-last shaped tools with the pottery indicates an influence from the Danubian culture further north, though the pottery itself is, of course, quite different. In Period II the country seems to have been overrun by the Schipenitz and Cucuteni painted-pottery folk. At Dimini occur large numbers of hand-made, shallow bowls narrowing at the base; these are painted inside and out in monochrome, geometric patterns being employed. There is also an incised ware, the decoration being done with deep firm lines. The third period in Thessaly shows influences from the Bronze Age cultures developing in the south. There also occurs a painted crusted ware, the paint on which was not burnt in when the pot was fired but can be removed by friction or washing. This is an important find as it makes it possible to correlate the industry of this period in Thessaly with that of Moravia where a similar painted

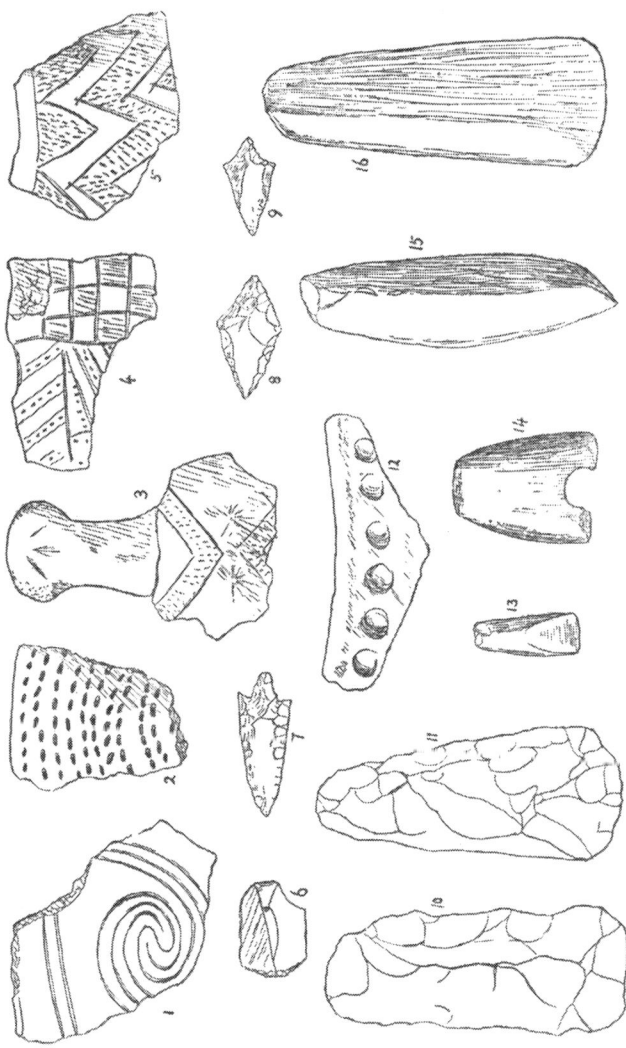

Plate 21. Examples of the industry found at Butmir (Bosnia).

ware developed at the end of Neolithic times. Perhaps it was an unsuccessful attempt to copy the splendid painted pottery ware of the Schipenitz type by a folk who had not yet learnt the method of firing pots already painted. The Moravian painted pottery is decorated with geometric patterns; a white or red paint being usually laid on a dark ground[1].

The fourth Thessalian period does not concern us here; the Mycenean culture from the south overran the whole region. These Thessalian cultures are very interesting and varied. Not only can the four main periods be determined, as at such sites as Dimini and Rakhmani, but in each period—except perhaps the last —there were certain local variations in both the shapes of the pots and the technique. For example, one local technique consists in decorating a pot not by adding paint but by scraping a pattern through the slip before firing, so as to show the colour of the underlying paste of which the pot had been made. The investigator is often able to tell with fair accuracy not only the age of a pot but the site whence it must have come.

Returning to the Painted Pottery folk themselves, no burials either in Thessaly or in Transylvania are as yet known, so we can say nothing about the race to which they belonged. The source of the culture and its relationships remain a mystery. The whole forms a rather restricted and very anomalous group. It may be remembered that painted pottery had been manufactured long before at Anau in Russian Turkestan and a very fine painted ware has been dug up from the earliest levels at Susa, as well as

---

[1] At this time in Moravia and some other districts an appliqué work mode of decoration for pottery was employed. The decoration was obtained not by engraved lines, but by a technique rather recalling the icing of a cake; the result is that the motifs stand up in high relief.

at other pre-Sumerian sites in Mesopotamia. Painted pottery is also found in the Neolithic industries of Egypt and China(8). But the motifs of this West Russian and eastern European group are not the same as those at Anau(9) or Susa(10), and at present we can do nothing but accept the existence of these people with their fine painted pottery culture and wait until further excavation supplies a clue as to their origin.

From Hungary there also comes a well-baked pottery decorated with fine engraved lines and simple geometric patterns. The age seems to be Late Neolithic but the origin of this variety is not yet clearly known.

A very important site about which a separate note is necessary is at Butmir near Serajevo, Bosnia(11). The industries are rather anomalous and their relationships not all quite certain. The age is Late Neolithic and no metal has been found. Butmir itself seems to have been a focus of culture with an influence that can be traced over a wide area. For example somewhat similar types of pottery have been excavated from Stone Age tumuli as far south as the Vardar valley above Salonika. The excavations at Butmir have exposed a land-village site, the industries including polished and chipped celts, shoe-last celts, perforated hammer axes, picks, tanged arrow heads, trimmed flakes, scrapers, hammer stones, etc. The pottery is often beautifully decorated with geometric patterns in fine lines or punctuations, etc. Spirals occur as a motif. There appear to be strong influences from the Pile-Dwelling cultures. A special feature is the large number of terra-cotta figurines that have been found. These represent the human form in a rather conventionalised way. Figurines of "goddesses" become commoner from Late Neolithic times onwards and form a widely spread group which occurs over a large part of the Near East[1]. Terra-cotta spindle whorls also come from Butmir. Although not belonging strictly to the Eastern Area series, its geographical situation makes it necessary to give this description here. Plate 21 will show examples of the finds.

BIBLIOGRAPHY AND REFERENCES

(1) V. G. CHILDE. *The Dawn of European History. 1925. (Ch. XII.)
(2) H. REINERTH. *Chronologie der jüngeren Steinzeit. Tübingen, 1924.
(3) J. PALLIARDI. "Die relative Chronologie der jüngeren Steinzeit in Mähren." Wiener Prähistorische Zeitschrift, I, 1914.
(4) WOSINSKI MOR. Das prähistorische Schanzwerk von Lengyel.
(5) M. M. VASSITS. Prähistorische Zeitschrift, Berlin.
(6) V. G. CHILDE. "Schipenitz: a Late Neolithic Station with painted pottery in Bukowina." Journ. Roy. Anth. Inst. vol. LIII, July–Dec. 1923. From this paper references to accounts of other sites belonging to the same culture can be obtained.
(7) A. J. B. WACE and M. S. THOMPSON. Prehistoric Thessaly. 1912.
(8) See bibliography (2) at end of chapter III.
(9) See bibliography (4) at end of chapter II.
(10) E. POTTIER. Mémoires de la Délégation en Perse. Tome XIII, Recherches Archéologiques, Céramique peinte de Suse.
(11) See bibliography (2) at end of chapter II.

[1] They occur too in the West as for example in Brittany.

CHAPTER VI

NEOLITHIC CULTURES OF THE NORTHERN AND WESTERN AREAS

HAVING briefly sketched out the story of the Neolithic development in eastern Europe, we must
now turn our eyes westwards. There are two districts,
a Northern and a Western, to be considered, but there
is close connection between them and they are more
conveniently treated in a single chapter.

The culture of the Western Area had a special development along the mountain backbone of the continent in
the shape of a Lake-Dwelling culture, which seems to be,
in part at any rate, an early hybrid between the Danubian
culture of the Eastern Area and that of the Western Area.

As a whole the Neolithic cultures of the Western
and Northern Areas owe considerably more to the Mesolithic folk who preceded them than is the case in eastern
Europe, where the Mesolithic is rarer and the Neolithic
culture was distinctly intrusive. So much is this the
case that it has been suggested that the older Mesolithic
cultures, transformed and become Neolithic by the
introduction of the fundamental discoveries that had
been made by true Neolithic man, formed a considerable
part of the Neolithic cultures of the Western and Northern Areas. It has been urged, further, that the great
megalithic tomb structures, that we shall describe
before long, are an attempt to reproduce artificially the
cave graves of a former time; certain it is that, though
the Mesolithic folk were probably few in numbers,
they must have contributed enormously to the new
culture, and further, it is not very easy to see exactly

how and whence a totally new people bringing the Neolithic civilisation from outside could have arrived. By the end of Danubian I times the Danubians had, it is true, penetrated as far as Belgium at any rate, and it is quite possible that this period is not far removed in time from the early true Neolithic times of western Europe and that while the Danubian peasant of Period I was cultivating the soil of the Lower Danube area, the Mesolithic hunter and fisher may still have been inhabiting the west. But that anything like an extensive intrusion of the Danubians into the Western and Northern Areas occurred is wellnigh impossible.

The Western and Northern Areas are linked together by the presence in both of megalithic constructions, and it will be necessary, therefore, before going further, to say a word or two about these monuments.

The simplest megalithic monument is the Menhir which consists of a single monolith set up, as a rule, at or near a burial spot. The monolith may be small or gigantic in height, examples being known as much as 30 feet high near Carnac in Brittany. Menhirs sometimes consist of natural stones of suitable shape; sometimes they are roughly shaped and squared, tapering towards the top. Some prehistorians have seen a phallic significance in certain instances; this may or may not be the case. Engravings on menhirs are known, though these are usually very rough and apparently of no very great significance.

Another construction is the Cromlech or stone circle of varying size and often found surrounding a menhir (Plate 22, no. 5). It is composed of a ring of large stones carefully placed. A series of alleys, formed by long lines of small menhirs covering an immense area of ground, are known; these are called Alignments.

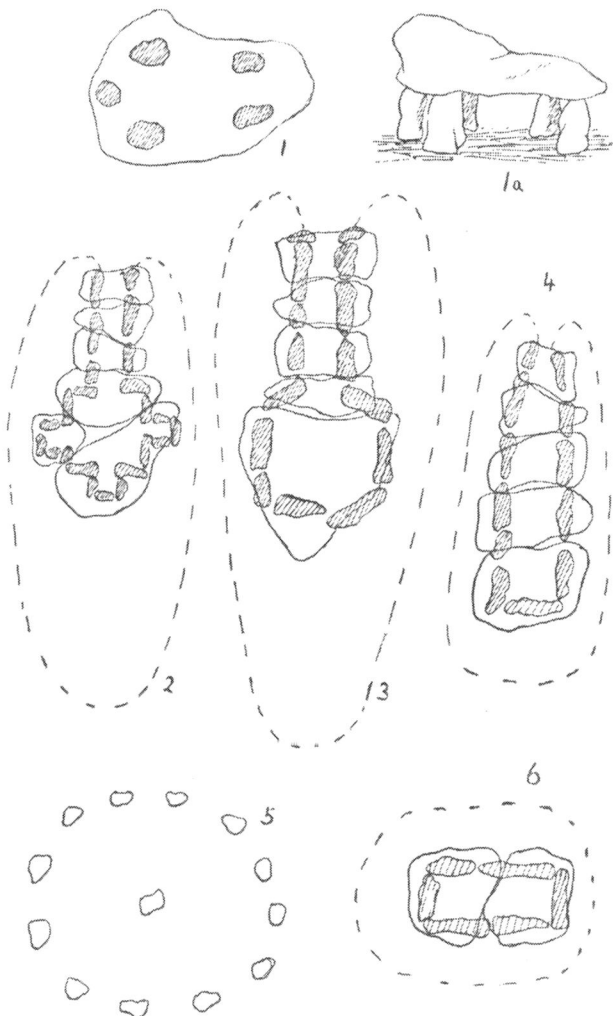

Plate 22. Sketches to show forms of megalithic constructions.

The most important yet discovered are those at Carnac in Brittany, where there are as many as ten alley-ways leading down from a large cromlech; they run in a straight direction for more than a quarter of a mile; then, after a short gap, turn slightly to the left and run on for some considerable distance, then after another gap, continue again a little further. The motive and use of these alignments is not known. That they were not built for an astronomical purpose, is seen by the fact that at Carnac they do not run in a straight line throughout, there being at least two bends in them. It has been suggested that the changes in direction are merely due to the fact that these alignments tend to follow a slight ridge of higher ground. In age they are somewhat newer than a large neighbouring menhir and the grave it marks, for recent work has shown a stratigraphical sequence between this grave, and the small menhirs of the alignment which strike straight across without regard to the earlier interment. However all menhirs are not of the same age, and these simple tombstones are found in many periods.

The most important megalithic structures are the Dolmen, the Passage Grave and the Stone Kist. The dolmen (Plate 22, nos. 1 and 1a) consists of a series of large stones upon which has been laid a huge slab of rock as a lid; the whole was covered by a mound of earth or tumulus which has often wholly or in part disappeared. Under the lid, in the chamber so formed, the body or bodies and the funeral furniture were buried. The lids are sometimes of enormous size and tremendous weight; how they were removed from the quarry to the site and placed on the uprights remains a mystery. That it was a matter of difficulty can be seen in the case of a large dolmen just south of Dublin, the lid of which is many tons in weight. The dolmen itself is situated at the bottom of a little valley, and the lid or cap-stone was apparently quarried high up on the valley side, so that all that was required was to lower it to the uprights below. But even this must have been no light task. In the case of another dolmen, the lid of which is smaller but by no means a feather-weight, found in South Wales near Cardiff, we can actually see the site near by whence the lid was quarried; but in this case the dolmen is not constructed below in a valley, and one can only remain amazed at the ability of these early folk to perform what even now would be quite a complicated mechanical task.

Passage Graves (Plate 22, nos. 2, 3, 4) may be considered as more or less elaborated and complicated dolmens. They consist of a chamber composed of large upright slabs, covered by a lid or cap-stone; from this chamber there emerges a passage, varying in length, itself composed of upright slabs roofed with flagstones; the whole covered with a tumulus or earth mound[1] (shown by dotted lines in the Plate). Between the sepulchral chamber and the passage there is sometimes placed a stone slab with a hole in it, large enough to admit a body. Such slabs are called port-hole entrances.

The Stone Kist (Plate 22, no. 6) may be regarded as being a degenerate form of Passage Grave, the chamber itself having disappeared, and the end of the passage acting as the burying place. Later these stone kists were made quite small and developed into glorified coffins.

[1] A variety has been found in France where the chamber consists of an artificially excavated cave in the hillside, reached by a passage of the usual kind.

In Scandinavia it can be shown that the dolmen is earlier than the passage grave or the stone kist but continues to exist up to Metal Age times. Later the passage grave, and finally, at the end of Neolithic times, the stone kist appears. The Spanish Peninsula is another good area for studying the development of these megalithic buildings, for here, especially in the south, we find a rich Copper Age from very early times, due partly to the influence of the progressive eastern Mediterranean folk and resulting in a very highly developed culture. At the end of the period there was a rapid and peculiar development in construction. We often find large passage graves where the sepulchral chamber has grown at the expense of the passage, with the result that, as at Cueva Menga for example, we find a chamber of enormous size, the gallery being merely a short and wide entrance passage. In the instance given the chamber measures over 25 metres long by rather more than 6 metres wide and nearly 3 metres high. There are central roof supports, and when it is remembered that this chamber was completely covered by only five lid-stones, something of the task accomplished by these primitive folk will be realised. Obviously building these gigantic constructions was no easy task, and a simplified method was later introduced which enabled the builders to form them without the difficulty of heaving the lid-stones up onto the uprights, and which also did away with the necessity of having uprights stout enough to support their weight. A suitable small hill was chosen on the top of which a wide trench was dug. At the bottom of this trench the lid-stones were laid and the whole then filled in. Excavation was then carried through the side of the hill under the lid-stones, and a chamber was hollowed out, care being taken that the chamber was always less in width than the lid-stones above, which therefore rested on undisturbed earth on either side. Finally a rough walling was built, often of small stones (dry walling), or thin slabs, that finished off the work; this last was for appearance rather than use as it had no weight to support.

At the end of the period in Spain we also note a new method of roof construction for the sepulchral chambers; corbelling (again a lazy way of avoiding the transport of large heavy lids or cap-stones) becomes common, doubtless due to influence from the east.

In England we have examples of most megalithic monuments, there being dolmens at Kidscot in Kent, also near Cardiff and elsewhere, passage graves (generally called "Long Barrows" on account of the oval shape of the tumuli) in many places on the mainland and in the Channel Islands, etc., and stone kists (generally called Round Barrows from the circular shape of the tumuli). Metal was already in use by the folk who made these barrows in our own land, and it is only in outlying areas, such as Scandinavia, where the introduction of metal for common use took place very late, that the stone kist can be considered as truly Neolithic.

The origin of the idea that led to the building of these megalithic tombs is a matter of great controversy, and it is by no means generally accepted that they represent a survival of Palaeolithic cave burials. Attempts have been made to trace their origin to Egypt. It has been pointed out that dolmens of all kinds flourish in the south of the Spanish Peninsula, are very common in Portugal (the dolmen field near Pavia(1) has yielded hundreds of examples), and that megalithic tombs have also been found in North-West Africa; the exponents

of the Egyptian theory therefore point triumphantly
to a complete chain following round the coast lines up
to Scandinavia. They are not found to any great extent
far away from coastal areas, in Central Europe for
example. But unfortunately there is a flaw in the argument; the North-West African examples have yielded
an industry belonging to the Iron Age! Again, it is
not fair to consider Spain as a mere intervening link,
for southern Spain, with its brilliant Copper Age culture, that grew up when the rich native ores were
exploited, was just as capable of initiating a new cult
as Egypt itself. The developments of the megalithic
monument in South Spain were far more elaborate
than those found further north, and if the Spanish
Peninsula received the idea from Egypt and passed it
on northwards, why did it not also pass on its discovery
of easier methods of construction? No, the origin of
these buildings remains a mystery. That they had a
splendid development in Spain is undoubted; that they
were widespread over western France is a fact; and
that they were introduced into the Northern Area from
the west is probable. All that can be said is that they
point to a definite cult of the dead, a desire to protect
bodies from the ravages of wild beasts and at the same
time from being crushed by the weight of a mound of
earth, which would have been the case if they had
merely been covered with a heap of stones or earth,
though simple burials under heaps of stones are sometimes found.

At the moment it is not possible to go further as to
their origin in western Europe; comparisons with somewhat similar constructions built for the same purpose
in far distant lands, such as India and other areas, but
of very different date, do not seem helpful. Somewhat

the same sort of argument must be used in the case of the dolmens as a whole as was used in the case of the pigmy stone industries. They indicate an idea which may well grow up at different times in different places in the spirit of mankind, but once this idea, namely protection of the body intact, neither crushed by over-laid stones nor free to be devoured by wild beasts, is introduced, the building of these tombs is a natural sequel. That these monuments, ultimately, had a ritual significance is shown by the continuance of their form even when no longer needed. Thus in England we sometimes find, at the end of long barrows, a portal that leads to no passage; the body being buried in a small chamber unconnected with the exterior.

The Neolithic civilisation introduced well-made polished stone axes into western Europe. As has been noted, these are not found in Mesolithic times and only begin to appear, for example, in the upper layers (that is the latest in date) of the shell mounds. These polished axes or celts vary to a certain extent in shape, and a definite evolution has been determined both for the Western and Northern Areas. They have been described in chapter IV.

Pottery was not unknown in certain Mesolithic industries, as, for example, in the Kitchen Midden and the Campignian, but with the coming of the true Neolithic civilisation the use of pottery was extended. Its manufacture was improved and a certain amount of decoration added. This, in Mesolithic times, had been of the very simplest, often merely a row or two of imprints left by the finger on the soft clay before firing.

Neolithic pottery in the west, however, was not made of such carefully prepared paste nor had it anything like the beauty of form or design that we find eastwards, among the Danubian folk, nor can it be compared with the beautiful contemporary productions of the eastern Mediterranean cultures. In the Northern Area, however, we can note the development of well-made and well-decorated pots, especially towards the end of the period. It is not fair to take the pottery of the early Swiss Lake-Dwelling culture as an example of ceramic art in Western Areas, as the Danubian culture itself played a very large part in its development. Reference should be made to chapter iv for shapes and decoration motifs found in these areas.

NORTHERN AREA(2)

In a previous chapter we have already noted the presence in Scandinavia and the Baltic areas of the Maglemosean culture replaced later by that of the Kitchen Middens; the Maglemosean probably continued to exist and develop in the hinterland, away from the coasts, and in other inhospitable regions, and formed what we call to-day the Arctic culture. The Kitchen Midden folk at an early date seem to have come under two influences, the one from the Western Area, which lay south of them, and the other perhaps from the east, though the exact direction is unknown. The former of these influences introduced the polished stone axe of the basal type already described and the idea of the megalithic tombs. The eastern development introduced at an early date into the Northern Area the so-called "comb" pottery, so named because its decoration was done with a tool resembling a comb (Plate 17, nos. 7, 11). However, as Åberg has pointed out to the author, a "comb" decoration is not at all uncommon; it is found on the pottery of the "Arctic" culture in Sweden and Finland as well as in several sites in Central Europe, etc. Nevertheless its appearance in the Northern Area fairly early in Neolithic times denotes a definite outside influence. Many prehistorians consider that there was an actual migration of some people westwards from an unknown cradle in northern Asia. Whether these influences alone were sufficient to develop the brilliant Neolithic civilisation of the north, or whether there was an actual replacement of inhabitants by new folks is not yet determined. The development of the polished stone celt and its association with various types of megalithic tombs[1] has been described in chapter IV. Associated with this celt began to appear the battle axe, whose connection will shortly be described. At the end of Neolithic times are found the beautifully made stone daggers and the large leaf-shaped javelin points that can be seen in so many museums; they were doubtless copies of metal weapons from the south.

From the end of Dolmen times onwards we have to note the existence, side by side with the regular megalithic tombs, of a new kind of burial in single-graves containing one body each and ringed with or covered by a heap of stones, the whole surmounted by a low mound of earth. These were first found in Jutland and were apparently due to the incursion of a new and warlike people who introduced the battle axe. It was not till after Passage-Grave times, however, that they dominated the whole of the Northern Area. German archaeologists consider that they were a native growth in the north whence they spread far and wide, dominating the folk of other areas when they came into contact with them on the disappearance of the primaeval forests of Central Europe. Professor Myres and his

[1] These tombs in Scandinavia have yielded as many as five types of skeletons, showing that the population was of a very mixed character.

school, on the other hand, consider that they originated in South Russia, where a number of such single-graves with the bodies buried in heaps of ochre have been found associated with the battle-axe type of weapon. The question is: was the movement from this South Russian area northwards an early one, or is this South Russian culture due to a late incursion from the north? Again, in Central Germany when the forests disappeared many hybrid forms arose, one of the most important of these being as we have seen the Corded Ware folk, who, before firing, decorated their pottery by impressing it with a twisted cord. These people, whose cradle was in Thuringia, certainly had close connections with the Battle-Axe folk and were themselves a warlike, dominating race. Are we to consider that their origin was due to hybridisation from the north, or, if we accept the South Russian area as the cradle of the Battle-Axe folk, are these Corded Ware people derived direct from the same cradle? Again we have divergent views between the two schools of archaeologists. Possibly both are partly true. It may be that the Battle-Axe people originated in South Russia and thence migrated north-west round the forests to settle on the shores of the Baltic; that they absorbed the Neolithic culture of the people there, and finally dominated them; that when the forests disappeared they spread southwards forming hybrids like the Rössen folk of the Merseburg district and the Corded Ware people. Their typical tool, the battle axe, has been found spread over a great part of northern Europe and indicates the wide extension of this warlike race. Perhaps we may for once reverse the usual process and use later history to explain earlier. In the ninth century of our own era the Swedes were a dominating people; they spread widely southwards and eastwards; organised the incoherent tribes of what is now Russia, and even took tribute from Byzantium. Anyone who has seen the great earthworks thrown up by these old Swedish warriors at such a place as Bielosersk in North Russia must admit the strength and virility of these Scandinavian conquerors. But Scandinavia, although it bred, then as always, a virile race, was not big enough and its climate not suitable for such a rapid increase of population as is necessary to control wide lands obtained by conquest. The result was that this early domination fell to pieces. Probably the same thing happened at the end of Early Neolithic times. Whether the Battle-Axe folk were developed around the shores of the Baltic *in situ*, or whether the stock was introduced from South Russia, their evolution did to a certain extent take place in this Northern Area during a considerable period of time; but when, at the end of Neolithic times, the climate permitted, and they spread and dominated far and wide, the increase of population was not sufficient to meet the requirements, with the result that their influence gradually waned [1].

[1] V. G. Childe does not stop at South Russia for a cradle, but sees the origin of the battle axe itself in certain weapons in Mesopotamia. Other archaeologists, however, are inclined to see a reverse movement. The question is a difficult one, and it must be added that between Mesopotamia and South Russia lies some very difficult and not easily traversed country. The pottery of the Northern Area is distinctive, the usual types being the large amphora and the collared flask which often has a ring where the collar and the body meet. Other types can be seen in the chapter on Typology. The collared flasks with rings are interesting, as a similar example, but having the ring of gold, has been found in South Russia.

THE WESTERN AREA(3)

The Western Area is in many ways distinct in its development from the Northern, due to the fact that a large part of what is now the north of Holland was in Neolithic times below the level of the sea, and that contact, although always possible, was not so easy as it would be to-day. The typical tool, the polished stone axe, develops differently, and the squaring of the edges and the flattening of the top and under surface are not seen to anything like the same extent: see chapter IV. Pottery in the Western Area never reached anything like the development that took place in the north, and although decoration was practised it was on the whole crude in comparison with that of the other areas. The only exception to this is in localities under the influence of the Mediterranean culture, but as here copper was already being used the culture is no longer really Neolithic. Even the wonderful developments at Carnac with their tumulus burials, alignments, beaker-pots, etc., so long classed as Late Neolithic, date from a time at the very extreme end of the true Neolithic period; in fact the finding of a certain amount of metal associated with the monuments has forced prehistorians to consider Carnac as definitely of Copper Age. Possibly the richness of Brittany was due to sea commerce in tin and callais (a rock rather like turquoise), and other minerals that were required by the more advanced Mediterranean folk who had already developed a sea trade.

In fact the cultural development over France and the Western Area generally in Neolithic times was rather dull and monotonous. The native decorated pottery is not very interesting and the series of polished stone celts becomes dreary. Little arrow heads, scrapers, knives, etc., of the usual types occur and plough-shares made of quartzite from the Forest of Montmorency have already been mentioned. The occurrence of handsome easily worked honey-coloured flint at Grand Pressigny (Indre et Loire) gave rise to a brisk commerce in this commodity, but it did not reach its climax till Copper Age times. The Omalian *fonds de cabanes* of Belgium have already been described. Some burials in a sort of stone kist at Chamblandes near Lausanne, of Middle to Late Neolithic date, are not without a certain interest. The Camp de Chassey, situated on the borders of the Departments of Saône et Loire and Côte d'Or, would seem to have been a well-fortified village. Some 800 yards long, with a breadth varying from 120 to 220 yards it occupied a strong position on the top of a narrow rocky plateau dominating the right bank of the River Dheune. Each end of the emplacement was protected by a raised embankment which in places is even now 15 yards high on the outside. The remains of habitations and hearths have been discovered as well as rich finds of pottery, implements, etc. The flint finds include scrapers, awls, fabricators, sickles and arrow heads in such quantities as to suggest their manufacture for trade. There are implements in polished stone, massive pierced stone rings, stone polishers and hones: bone points, stag antler hafts for tools, also small cups beautifully made from the base of the antler. Finally there is an immense variety of pottery; there are vases with saucer-like stands, small twin cups, spoons, and an infinity of bowls and vessels (Plate 16, nos. 4–7, 11, 12). The decorations are varied, some recalling those on Laibach pottery. The date of the village would seem to be Late Neolithic, though it continued to be used sporadically till the Iron Age[4].

SWISS LAKE DWELLINGS(s)

The Swiss Lake-Dwelling and the Pile-Village culture as a whole, found on both sides of the Alps stretching from eastern France right away through Austria and on into Jugo-Slavia, is of very special interest. A description of the pile dwellings has already been given in the chapter on Neolithic civilisation, and it only remains here to discuss the industries found and the origin and connection of the culture itself. The brilliant work of Vouga in recent years has determined a definite stratigraphy in the peat and mud under some of these Lake-Dwelling villages. Four distinct cultures have been determined. In the first of these occur beautifully made pottery, recalling the Danubian, and well-made stone axes, often from very choice rocks, such as serpentine, that must have been imported from some distance; these little polished stone axes are often mounted in the hollowed-out ends of portions of antler. Quite clearly there is a distinct connection with the later phases of Danubian I culture, although it would seem probable that the connection is not so much racial as an influence acting possibly on older Mesolithic folk who certainly existed previously in these regions, as has been proved by the finding of an Azilian station south of Basle at a site called Birseck, and elsewhere. In the second period, according to the stratigraphy of the Swiss Lake Dwellings, there was a very distinct falling off and the Danubian influence ceased. Possibly a more distinct influence from the Western Area can be traced. Between the first and second periods, owing to climatic changes, great floods occurred and the lakes rose. No cultural connection, therefore, is traceable between them. In the second period the implements were generally made from local rocks, and they and the pottery are of very inferior manufacture. In the third level there is distinct improvement and foreign rocks were again imported for the making of small polished tools. In the fourth or latest stage we note the introduction of copper, and the extensive commerce that grew up in parts of Europe at this time brought to the Swiss lake dwellers the especially valued dark honey-coloured flint from Grand Pressigny (West France).

The extension of the Pile-Dwelling culture along the foot-hills of the Alps on both sides of the central chain is of great interest, and the question arises: was the movement from the west eastwards; was the connection of Loubliana (Laibach) with Switzerland; or are we to look further east for the relationships and an east to west movement? On the whole, in Switzerland at any rate, there seems little need to postulate the introduction of a new racial element, and it does not seem inconceivable that much of the culture of the Pile Dwellings further east may be of autochthonous growth, undergoing influences to a greater or lesser extent from the Danubian industries of the loess lands. Laibach, itself contemporary with and in a way similar to, though different from the Pile-Dwelling cultures of the Mondsee in Austria, is late in time and must be considered in connection with the movement at the end of Neolithic times that brought together the various cultures, forming hybrids which themselves played a considerable part in the development of the peoples around.

No burials belonging to the Pile-Dwelling culture have as yet been discovered.

BIBLIOGRAPHY AND REFERENCES

(1) V. CORREIA. "El Neolítico de Pavia." *Mem. comm. de invest. pal. y prehist.* num. 27 (1921).

(2) N. ÅBERG. **Das Nordische Kultur Gebiet in Mitteleuropa während der jüngeren Steinzeit.* Uppsala, 1918.
S. MÜLLER. "L'Âge de la Pierre en Schlesvig." *Mém. de la Soc. Antiq. du Nord,* Copenhagen, 1913–14.

(3) A passage country lying between the Northern and Western Cultural Areas was the Netherlands. For a description of the Stone Age there see:
N. ÅBERG. *Die Steinzeit in den Niederlanden.* Uppsala, 1916.
J. DÉCHELETTE. **Manuel d'Archéologie préhistorique....* Vol. I. Paris, 1908. The chapters on the Neolithic period still remain very important for the student.
See also bibliography (2) at end of chapter v.

(4) Those wishing detailed studies on the Western Area cultures should consult:—
P. BOSCH GIMPERA. "Les civilisations de la Péninsule Ibérique pendant le Néolithique et l'Énéolithique," *L'Anthropologie,* tome xxxv, 1925, nos. 5–6: "Études sur le Néolithique et l'Énéolithique de France," *Revue Anthropologique,* 1926, nos. 7–9.
It should be noted that in the latter work the Campignian culture is classed as Early Neolithic. It should be recalled, however, that the Neolithic Civilisation in the west was due rather to the introduction of new ideas than of actual hordes of Neolithic folk. These ideas enabled the old Mesolithic stocks to become "Neolithicised" and permitted an increase in population which rapidly followed naturally according to the Malthusian Law.

(5) See bibliography (2) at end of chapter v.
See also bibliography (1) at end of chapter II.
P. VOUGA. "Essai de classification du Néolithique lacustre d'après la stratification." Three articles in the *Anzeiger für Schweizerische Altertumskunde,* Band XXII, Heft 4, 1920; and in the same journal for 1921 and 1922.

CHAPTER VII

A BRIEF SKETCH OF ENGLAND IN MESOLITHIC, NEOLITHIC, AND EARLIEST METAL AGE TIMES

I T has never been the purpose of this book to go into any kind of detail, and even in this chapter dealing with a restricted special area little more than a framework for more detailed study will be attempted. The problems of these post-Palaeolithic prehistoric cultures are very intricate, and there is seldom a well attested stratigraphy to assist the investigator.

It seems probable that in Late Palaeolithic times England, like Moravia and other parts of eastern Europe as well as Mentone and South Spain, had been peopled by the Aurignacian race but was never actually inhabited by Magdalenian man, whose cradle and focus appears to have been to the west in France. The influence of this glorious French culture was, however, felt far and wide[1], indeed isolated finds of true Magdalenian type have been recognised here and there in our own country; especially in the cave area of the south-west, but also as far north as Creswell Crags on the border line between Nottinghamshire and Derbyshire. England was no very suitable land for mankind at this date, especially the eastern parts[2] that remained long under the direct

[1] The Aurignacian culture developed in England contemporary with, and influenced by, the Magdalenian culture of France is sometimes called "Provincial Magdalenian."

[2] An Upper Palaeolithic industry similar to that found at Belloy-sur-Somme (France) has been noted in East Anglia and at North Cray in Kent.

influence of the Scandinavian icefields. However, Upper Palaeolithic culture as a whole seems to show a simple evolution from an original Aurignacian stock, and at Creswell Crags recent investigation would seem to indicate a direct evolution to something recalling Mesolithic industries(1). A small but interesting industry, comprising core scrapers, burins, blades and points (though without the Tardenoisean burin) has been lately found by Miss Layard one to two feet below the surface at a site in the Colne Valley. This industry probably also belongs to the very late Upper Palaeolithic development.

Occurrences of Azilian culture in West Yorkshire near Settle, on the shore at Whitburn near Newcastle, in the River Dee near Kirkcudbright, and in West Scotland, at Oban and on the island of Oronsay, have been noted. These are extremely anomalous finds, and it is by no means easy to see how such examples link on with the culture of the Pyrenees. The nearest connecting link is a not very typical harpoon found near Liège in Belgium, which connects it with typical industries found just south of Basle(2).

The West Yorkshire site near Settle is in Victoria Cave, which was excavated with great care towards the end of the nineteenth century, almost every object being carefully mapped on to a sort of latitude and longitude framework, so that it is almost possible to reconstruct the whole deposit to-day as it was before it was dug. Unfortunately, however, at the time of the excavations the effects of burrowing animals were not recognised, and for practical purposes the results from a stratigraphical point of view are perfectly useless. The deposits themselves are not horizontal, but at the back of the cave the floor level rises with the result that the burrowing animals, which abound, had only to excavate horizontally to intermix objects on the bottom layer with those from the top. Thus we find bones of cave bear from the basal level, not to speak of a hippopotamus bone weathered almost to a pebble, intermixed with Romano-British objects at the top of the deposit; while at the base, below Glacial deposits, are found bones clearly cut by a metal tool! Only two definite occupation layers can be recognised: a top one, Romano-British in date, that has yielded much rich enamelled work, and an under layer with but few objects, the age of which is difficult to determine. An Azilian harpoon (Plate 1, fig. 1*a*), very definite and typical, though without any attachment hole through the centre of the base of the stem, was found at the mouth of the cave in a talus from this lower level. That nothing can be hoped from stratigraphy at this site is further attested by the fact that a carved bone bead of Late Celtic date was found close to the harpoon. The difference in the preservation of the two objects is marked. The bead still contains a certain quantity of organic matter whereas the harpoon has become completely fossilised.

The finds at Oban are still more definitely Azilian. There are two sites, the one, called MacArthur's Cave, was discovered as long ago as 1894 during quarrying operations, it is near the centre of the modern town; the other is a rock shelter at Drumvaig—a suburb of Oban—now in the back yard of a row of tenement houses.

There have been considerable earth movements affecting the coast line of West Scotland in comparatively recent times, geologically speaking, and the cliff in which MacArthur's Cave was situated—it has been almost completely quarried away now for building purposes—has always been considered as marking an old sea shore. The section in the cave was as follows: at the top shingle, which covers a layer of black earth in which two long-headed skulls were found. Underneath this black layer occurred the main archaeological deposit comprising a sort of midden mixed with ashes and some sea sand. An industry consisting of scrapers, flakes, etc., as well as bone awls and harpoons, was collected. The latter were made of deer's antler and were for the most part of good size, the largest measuring some six inches in length, having four barbs on each side of the stem, and being pierced with an oval hole through the centre of the base of the stem, for attachment purposes. Some of the other and smaller examples, as in the case of the example from Victoria Cave, Settle, have no attachment hole.

It is important to realise the significance of the fact that sea sand was found intermixed with the main archaeological layer, for the sea to-day lies some 30 feet below the level of the site of MacArthur's Cave, and 100 yards or so away. Again, the shingle layer covering the black earth deposit must have been blown in by storms at a time when the cave stood near the high-water-mark level. The earth movements, then, that caused this raised beach of West Scotland must be subsequent to the inhabitation of MacArthur's Cave by Mesolithic man; they would seem, therefore, to be no older than the Neolithic Age.

Somewhat similar finds have been discovered in the island of Oronsay. They consist of at least five shell mounds or middens, the most important being locally called Caisteal-nan-Gillean. This site consists of a hillock some 150 feet in diameter and 25 feet high, the upper layers of which are composed of sands with a covering of turf and the archaeological deposit is only some eight feet in thickness. This deposit, consisting of ashes and sand, has yielded, besides quantities of shells, limpets, etc., an industry similar to that of MacArthur's Cave, including eleven harpoons said to have been lost at the Fishery Exhibition in London in 1883. Except that bones of the great auk occur, the fauna of those days appears to have been the same as that of mediaeval times.

Tardenoisean culture spread over our country, and persisted late. It is not always easy to determine whether a given pigmy industry is really Tardenoisean or Early Neolithic in date; H. Warren claims to have found in very Late Neolithic or Copper Age cultures geometric types, but without the typical tools. Probably Tardenoisean in culture are finds from Constantine Bay, near Padstow(3), North Cornwall; near Brighton(4); at Hastings(5); at Aberystwith; on the Pennines(6); near the coast of Northumberland and Durham where the few sites that are known are about a quarter of a mile inland from the present coast line (7). Pigmy industries have been found in Surrey, Sussex, at Land's End, on the Cleveland Hills and at many other sites, but the culture is uncertain. There is some doubt as to whether the microliths found in East Anglia and Lincolnshire should be assigned to the Tardenoisean or to the Maglemosean culture. The most important and carefully studied of these areas is that of the Pennines between Rochdale, Manchester and Huddersfield, where the chain narrows and sites are therefore concentrated (Plate 23). At a time when the lowlands were doubtless filled with forests, this upland area must have been fairly suitable for habitation. Various sites have been excavated by F. Buckley. They consist for the most part of workshop "floors" on the tops of hillocks, the actual height above sea level varying from 1000–1500 feet. Two distinct types of industry have been noted, the one —on stratigraphical grounds judged to be slightly later than the other—closely connected with the Tardenoisean culture of Belgium, the other probably more local in origin. This sequence, however, is based solely on what was found in an excavation at a single site on the north side of Warcock Hill, Marsden (Yorkshire), where the two industries are in contact, and further evidence is required before the matter can be conclusively proved. Both industries comprise small scrapers, trimmed flakes and various pigmy tools; the difference between the two is mainly that the later industry, which is rare, contains broad flakes and tools, no angle gravers but abundant Tardenoisean ones, while in the earlier or local series the implements and flakes are narrow, Tardenoisean gravers are absent but the angle type though rare does occur. Almost all these workshop sites had a small hearth; and burnt flints and carbonised wood, that can sometimes be identified as oak, birch, etc., have been collected. While the newer broad-blade industry is undoubtedly closely related to the Tardenoisean culture of Belgium, the earlier local series may be compared with the final developments of the British Upper Palaeolithic culture, the first phases of which, at any rate, are to be seen in the top levels at Creswell Crags. It is certainly true that in the narrow-blade series a number of pigmy shouldered points are found corresponding somewhat to similar finds at Creswell and in the upper levels at Mentone where a rather similar evolution of the Aurignacian culture seems to have been going on. To the east of the Pennines in South-East

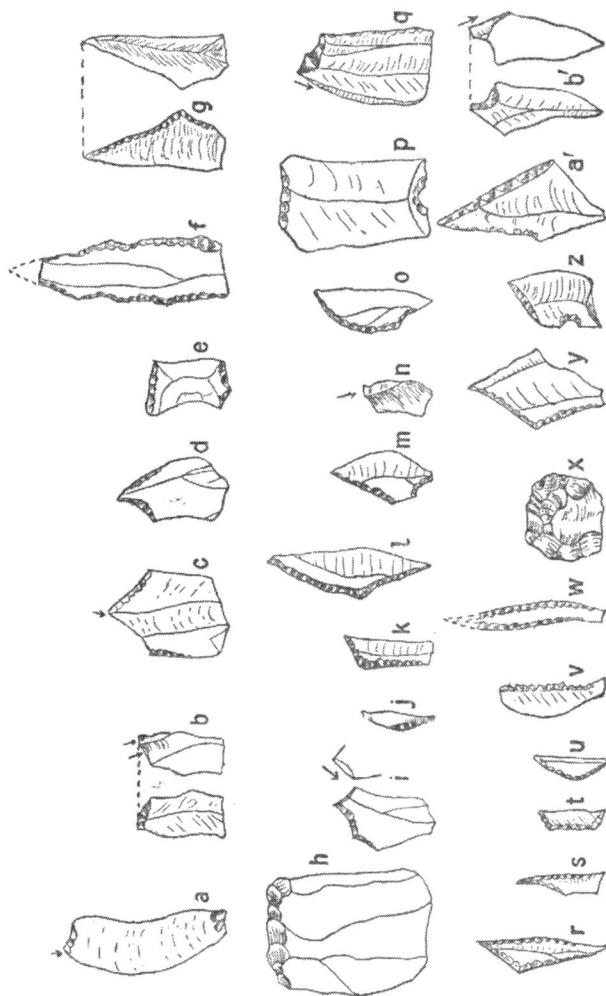

Plate 23. English Tardenoisean industries from: W. Yorkshire and Pennines near Marsden (a–j). Peacehaven near Brighton (k, l, m). Hastings (n). Bamburgh (o, p). Narrow-blade industry from the Marsden district (r, s, t, u, v, w, x). Broad-blade industry from the Marsden district (y, z, a′, b′–g).

Yorkshire two Maglemosean harpoons and a stone industry have been discovered(8). The situation is therefore of very great interest; to the west of the Pennines we have Azilian, on the hills Tardenoisean, and to the east Maglemosean industries. One day, perhaps, a definite stratigraphy will give us the relation of the three to one another. Pigmy tools, but without gravers, are found at Scunthorpe in Lincolnshire, as well as further south over the sandy areas and "brecks" of Norfolk and Suffolk. These pigmy tools sometimes show a very deep and apparently old patina, and it is not impossible that some at any rate will be found to belong to the Maglemosean culture (Plate 24). At the flint mines at Grimes Graves (Norfolk) a stratigraphical sequence has been in part made out by L. Armstrong, who has discovered a certain amount of art in the older layer. This consists for the most part of rather meaningless lines scratched on flint crust; but in one case a not badly drawn deer is figured. The technique, however, cannot be described as Palaeolithic, and it may be that this early industry at Grimes Graves is also of Maglemosean or possibly of "Arctic" culture, which, as has been seen, is closely connected with the Maglemosean, though rather later in time.

Coming to post-Mesolithic times we are enabled, thanks to the researches of H. Warren, to call geological evidence to our aid and so obtain a sort of stratigraphical sequence in the low-lying areas of Essex(9). It appears that at some moment in Neolithic times a land submergence set in with the result that the land sank below the level of the sea. This is just the reverse of what took place along the coast line of the west of Scotland, as has just been seen above.

An ideal section—never yet seen in its entirety, but

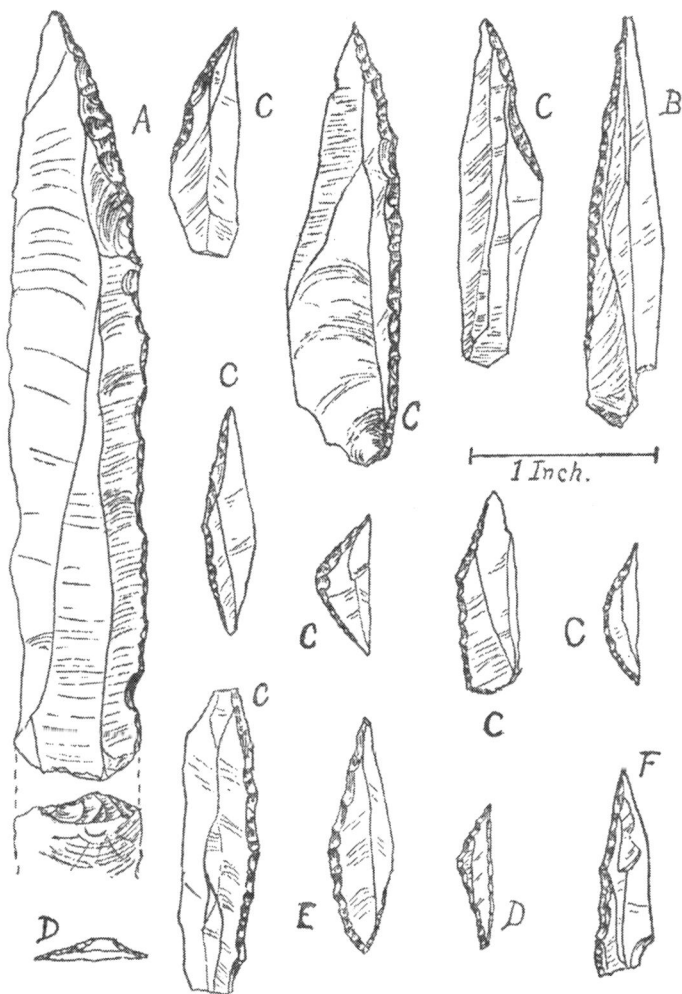

Plate 24. East Anglian small industries from: (A) Brandon; (B) Kenny Hill; (C) Lakenheath; (D) Scunthorpe; (E) Undley [all in Camb. Museum]; (F) Weston near Stevenage.

deduced from a combination of various sections is as follows:—

Re-emergence of the land	Present salting surface	
Land below sea level	Tidal silt or scrobicularia clay	
Land sinking	Peat	
Land sinking	Buried prehistoric sites surface	Beaker folk industry
	Rainwash = locally grey marsh clay	Neolithic industry with arrow heads
	Pleistocene brickearths	

Other important sites in this connection are on the coasts of northern Ireland in Antrim, Londonderry, etc. A good example is at Whitepark Bay[10]. The geological situation resembles that in Scotland, there having been a considerable submergence of the land in very early post-Glacial times and re-emergence in Late Mesolithic times. On this re-elevated land surface lived Neolithic man, as is evidenced by the finding of great quantities of rough tools—cores, scrapers, flakes, chipped axes and the like. By the River Bann many small chipped flints have been collected which at first recall a Mesolithic industry. No burins occur, however, and H. Warren claims that similar industries, with typical Late Neolithic or Earliest Metal Age types, occur sporadically in Essex, and so these River Bann specimens are probably also to be classed as Late Neolithic in age. A peculiar type of tool is also found in the same locality. This consists of a broad, flat, pointed flake, having at the base a short stout central tang. The tool resembles a coarse arrow head without any secondary working except around the tang. This type has not been recognised elsewhere in Neolithic industries (Plate 14, no. 3).

Neolithic man has left for us, as evidence of his culture, stone industries, and more rarely pottery, mines where the raw material for tool making was procured, and burials in megalithic constructions known ordinarily as "Long Barrows." The stone industries are for the most part surface finds and comprise the usual celts, fabricators, scrapers, awls, arrow heads, etc. They occur commonly on the sandy upland regions of Suffolk and Norfolk overlooking the Cambridgeshire fens; they are not found in the former forest lands and hardly even along the river valleys. As has been pointed out in a previous chapter the Neolithic celt starts by having a circular section at the butt end, while at the dawn of the Metal Age the tool became flatter and consequently the section through the butt more oval. Both varieties are found in East Anglia and it may therefore be presumed that the whole of Neolithic times is represented by these surface finds. However the matter is not quite simple, and certain tools, at any rate, will probably be found to be older and to belong to the Mesolithic period. On the other hand flint was in use in England until Iron Age times and, without stratigraphy to help the investigator, it is often almost impossible to be certain of the Neolithic date. True Neolithic pottery is rarely found in this country, though a few examples have been found in some *fonds de cabanes* near Peterborough excavated by Wyman Abbott(11). Neolithic pots have also come from the Thames, as for example a beautifully decorated vessel with a round bottom from Mortlake (Plate 16, no. 9), and once or twice fragments have been found in long barrows.

Flint mines whence prehistoric man obtained the raw material necessary for his tool making have been found in several places in England; they approximate in type to that of St Gertrude, South Holland, already described in chapter III. The two most important flint mines in England are those at Grimes Graves (Norfolk), and at Cissbury (Sussex). Crossing the railway line at Brandon station, take the right hand road towards Mundford. After a mile or so, again take the right-hand fork and half-way between it and a little wood seen ahead take a cart track to the right which more or less follows a shallow valley in the heath. A mile or so ahead, just to the right of the shallow valley, a coppice is seen, this is Grimes Graves(12). In the coppice one finds numerous shallow cup-like depressions, which are the nearly filled up shafts—originally some forty feet or so deep—that were sunk to tap the flint-bearing strata of chalk and from the bottom of which radiated horizontal galleries as at St Gertrude. The so-called "floors" where the raw chunks of flint were roughly trimmed, lie along the edge of the shallow valley already mentioned. A certain amount of stratigraphical evidence has been accumulated showing that these floors are not all contemporary and that two ages can be demonstrated. Some rough scratched lines, as well as a quite well-drawn engraving of a deer, on pieces of flint crust were collected from the earlier industry. These have already been mentioned in another connection. They may be connected with the Maglemosean or its descendant the Arctic culture, though examples of rough scratched lines were also observed at another mine (or rather prehistoric quarry) and factory site in North Wales at Penmaenmawr which is of Neolithic date(13). The industries at Grimes Graves have been claimed as Palaeolithic, in part at any rate, and it has been urged that flint mines existed at this site as early as Mousterian times. A miner's bag of tools is not "home" furniture, and the industries, comprising as they do tools useful for extraction of the raw material in the mines themselves and their subsequent rough trimming at the "floors" or factory sites, would lead us to expect rather unusual types of tools. There is really nothing peculiarly Palaeolithic, Neolithic types occur and the fauna is modern. At the Cissbury mines a chalk lamp was discovered placed on a shelf of chalk so as to light the miner at his work.

For Neolithic burials we must turn to the so-called "Long Barrows"(14) which occur most frequently in the counties of Wiltshire and Gloucestershire and their surrounding districts. Such barrows are elongated oval mounds frequently pointing east and west, being higher and broader at the eastern end. The body or bodies were placed in a chamber built of large blocks of stone and approached by a similarly built passage with sometimes a door or portal on the outside. In other words we are dealing with the "passage grave" or its derivative. A good example of a long barrow occurs at West Kennet near Avebury (Wiltshire). Here the barrow, 336 feet long by 75 feet wide at the eastern end, was originally surrounded by a line of upright stones, the intervals between which were filled up by horizontal courses of dry-walling. Some of the stone slabs forming the roof of the passage and chamber under the eastern end of the barrow weighed about a ton each. Four long-headed skeletons were found in the chamber, also some scraps of Neolithic pottery. These four persons may have been the original tenants of the barrow, but unfortunately it must have been reopened, possibly more than once, as apparently later pottery and other bones were also found. In the Cotswolds the dry-walling edging sometimes forms a heart-shaped rather than an oval ground-plan at the eastern end. Such a case is "Hetty Pegler's Tump" at Uley (Gloucestershire) excavated by Dr Fry in 1821. Originally four chambers opened from the central passage, 22 feet long, which was terminated by a low portal only three feet high but roofed by an enormous stone lintel 8 feet long and $4\frac{1}{2}$ feet thick. This doorway is in the middle of the eastern end, where the incurving heart-shaped walls meet. Several skeletons of mixed dates were found—two of the crania were sent to Guy's Hospital museum. An interesting fact about the skeletons found in these barrows is that they do not seem to have been placed there immediately after death. Indeed occasionally, as at Pole's Wood South (Gloucestershire), the chamber is too small to have contained the complete bodies of the skeletons had they been so interred. In other words these tombs were in many cases mere ossuaries. Cremation does not occur. It must be noted that sometimes one barrow contains several chambers, with possibly incomplete passages, and that often the doorway seems to have become merely symbolic as it has sometimes been found as a purely external structure leading to no chamber behind. Large stone doorways to the chamber itself, pierced with a hole big enough to admit a body and called "porthole" entrances, are fairly common on the continent but rare in England. Frequently the covering mound or tumulus has, to a greater or less extent, disappeared, leaving the large stones standing naked, thus giving a somewhat dolmen-like impression. A Late Neolithic date is generally admitted for these barrows, a few scraps of Neolithic pottery, arrow heads and javelin points, but never metal, having been found with the primary interments.

Another kind of barrow of circular form is frequently

found in England. These are called "Round Barrows." They are, however, of later date often containing cremation burials of a round-headed folk associated with Bronze Age industries. They appear to correspond with the stone kist as there is no passage to the internal chamber which is generally completely closed. But all megalithic monuments are not necessarily graves, even though they may be connected therewith, and their purposes have given rise to much speculation. Such monuments are the stone circle at Avebury (Wiltshire), the Deer Park near Sligo (Ireland) and of course the classic example of Stonehenge, about which a few words must now be said(15).

Originally Stonehenge must have consisted of (1) a surrounding earthwork circle approached from the north-east by a similar avenue, (2) an outer circle of local, so-called "sarcen" stones with lintels joining their tops. These lintels were held in place by tenons on the uprights and corresponding sockets on the under surfaces of the crosspieces, while each lintel was secured to its neighbour by a similar groove and ridge joint. (3) an inner circle of smaller upright "blue stones"— a rock foreign to the district, (4) five great sarcen tri-lithons arranged to form a horseshoe, opening towards the avenue. The largest central trilithon must have been some 25 feet high, (5) an inner horseshoe of upright "blue stones," (6) the altar stone, a large recumbent slab, 16 feet by 3 feet 4 inches, placed in the arch of the "blue stone" horseshoe on the so-called axis. This axis is an imaginary straight line passing from the centre of the middle trilithon, through the centre of the circle and out down the earthwork avenue. Unfortunately of course a very large number of the stones are no longer in position. Besides these stones belonging to the main building there are, or were, some half-dozen isolated ones variously placed with reference to the circle. Of these four, or rather two now existing ones and the holes where two others must have been, are to be found just within the surrounding earthwork. They are arranged symmetrically, each occupying a position the same distance from the centre of the circle and each making an angle of 22½ degrees with that diameter of the building which cuts the axis at right angles. Each pair thus makes an angle of 45 degrees at the centre of the circle. Then there are the "Slaughter Stone" and "Hele Stone," which stand in the avenue but not centrally. There has been much unproductive controversy as to the purpose of the latter. It now seems fairly certain that the blue stones of which the inner circle and horseshoe are formed must have been brought from the Prescelly mountains in Pembrokeshire. They are made of a rock quite foreign to Wiltshire and Dr H. Thomas says that no other area in Britain except Prescelly can meet all the requirements necessary as a source of supply for these Stonehenge megaliths(16). Also it can hardly be coincidence that the Prescelly neighbourhood is very rich in stone circles, etc., and was clearly a sacred area. As regards a possible date for the erection of Stonehenge, opinions vary, some assigning it to the end of the Neolithic or beginning of the Copper Age. No tools really helpful for dating purposes have been found, and we may dismiss, as not giving any conclusive evidence, a small copper stain on a stone which was once made much of by archaeologists. Neither does the complete absence of metal tools prove a Neolithic date, as even in the Copper Age such precious and somewhat soft implements would hardly have been used for the rough work of dressing the stones. Again various cremations have been found around, in one case in the hole for one of the four symmetrically placed stones mentioned above, and here, though the cremation is of a later date than the Neolithic period, it is difficult to deduce any satisfactory theory therefrom. Lastly the all-important question of the direction of the axis must be noted. It has often been observed by persons standing behind the central trilithon and looking down the avenue that this axis seems to be directed to the point on the horizon at which the midsummer sunrise takes place. As a matter of fact this is not strictly so, and observations and calculations as accurate as fallen stones, etc. permit, have shown by how much it is incorrect. But this point of the midsummer sunrise has for some time been moving slowly eastwards at a rate approximately known, and it is therefore possible to arrive at a date when the direction of the Stonehenge axis would have been correct. Such a date is given as about B.C. 1840 or, allowing for the maximum of possible error, between B.C. 2040 and B.C. 1640. It is considered more than probable that the builders of the monument did intend their axis direction to be correct, and this may perhaps give us some clue as to the possible purpose of the building. Religiously it may have marked the northern limit of the "Sun God's" path, or more practically, may have had calendar-like uses very helpful to primitive agriculturists. At any rate the vicinity of Stonehenge was long regarded as a sacred area, for many barrows of the Bronze Age have been discovered in the neighbourhood.

A distribution map of the Neolithic cultures in England is very instructive, as we note how dependent these folk were on forest growth. Sites occur thickly on the sandy borders of the fen country in

Suffolk and Norfolk, where game of many kinds was plentiful; agriculture was little practised, as is evidenced by the almost complete absence of sickles. The hinterland on the "brecks" and warrens doubtless provided a scanty but sufficient pasturage for the few flocks. Even the valleys of the fen rivers were hardly occupied, and the great mass of the country contains scarcely any remains of these people(17). Most of the Midlands and the western border of England proper were also uninhabited, and in Late Neolithic and Early Metal Age times, when considerable movements of people took place westwards, it was North and South Wales that received independent contributions from the east, the whole of the central district remaining barren. Doubtless these forest lands were unsuitable for human existence in Neolithic times.

England was not wholly neglected by the Battle-Axe folk and examples of their axes occur; but the chief event that took place at the end of Neolithic times was the arrival of a new folk called the Beaker people, whom we have already mentioned in chapter v. Apparently cradled in Spain the culture spread over large parts of Europe, though the industries show certain variations in different districts. It was our eastern shores that were first invaded and the immigration seems to have come by way of the Rhine. It is important to note that the type of beaker found in Brittany is absent or very rare in England and that it was certainly not by that route that the culture was introduced into this country. The invaders differed somewhat from the former inhabitants of the land. The Neolithic folk seem to have been of moderate stature, long-headed, oval-faced, narrow-nosed, with small features. They were not at all a powerfully built race. The new-comers

on the other hand—according to Abercromby(18)—
were characterised by a short square skull showing a
great development of the superciliary ridges and eye-
brows. The cheek-bones, nose and chin were prominent
and the powerful lower jaw was supplied with large
teeth. They were a tall, strongly built race and must
have presented—at any rate as far as the men were
concerned—a fierce, brutal appearance. The dead were
buried in round barrows, inhumation being practised.
They knew about the use of copper and introduced into
England the beaker type of pot (Plate 19). These are
often beautifully decorated by means of a sort of cogged-
wheel tool, the pattern running in zones round the pot. But
the ornamentation was also often incised with a pointed
instrument and combinations show beautiful and complicated motifs. For the most part the beakers had no
handles, but a few handled cups ornamented with
characteristic decoration have been collected. These
may be connected with variations which were produced
in Central Europe in Beaker Age times. Abercromby
distinguishes three main types of beaker common in
England. Each of these types can in turn be sub-
divided—a matter of considerable local importance.
Although these people introduced copper, they still
manufactured most of their tools from flint, and scrapers,
arrow heads and the like—often beautifully made—
have been found. It is the opinion of the writer that
the glassy or waxy appearance often seen on some of
the finely made scrapers, "slugs," etc., due to fine
ripple markings on each facet caused by the use of
pressure flaking technique, can be taken as indicating
the presence of the Beaker culture. This is sometimes
helpful in determining whether a given industry is to
be classed as of Neolithic or of Beaker Age. The glassy

or waxy appearance on the tools was very marked in the case of some Beaker Age interments in a barrow at Barton Mills, excavated by Dr Cyril Fox in 1924(19). It must not be considered, however, as a *sine qua non* for all tools made by the Beaker folk. The immense majority of English beakers, generally associated with burials, are found in the eastern part of the island(20). But examples are found in Wiltshire and in South Wales, and a specimen has also been described from Baroose farm, Lonan parish, Isle of Man—its unusual flattened and decorated lip showing "Food vessel" influence of the Bronze Age[1]. One or two have also been discovered in Co. Down, Northern Ireland, and some further examples have been found in North Wales and a number in the Peak district. In East Anglia the Beaker folk, as did their Neolithic forerunners, preferred the high sandy lands overlooking the fens where food was easily obtainable, and it would seem that, arriving as invaders, they in part displaced the older inhabitants. It is in Beaker Age times that the fen islands were for the first time inhabited properly, and the theory that the old inhabitants were driven by the new-comers to take up their abode in less favourable and more fever-stricken quarters is plausible. Honey Hill near Manea is a good site for studying this question, as a rich industry, by all appearances contemporary but comprising Beaker folk examples among the numerous Neolithic types, has been collected there. At various sites in Scotland, as for example the Culbin sands and Cruden Bay (Aberdeenshire), tiny scrapers and well-made arrow heads, associated with "whorls"

---

[1] Certain "scribed" stones have also been published. The carving consists of a series of grooves intercrossing and running in all directions over the rocks. A few more definite figures, including a spiral, do, however, occur. No certain age can be assigned for this art group (21).

and small polished celts, sometimes pierced with a small hole for suspension purposes, have been found. The date of these industries is uncertain, but a very early Metal Age is probable. The Beaker folk never obtained a permanent footing in this country; after a time they simply seem to have merged with the older folk, though their influence continued to affect the original Neolithic stock which seems to have come again into its own. This has been rather neatly shown by R. Smith, of the British Museum, in a study of the evolution of a particular kind of pot dating from the Bronze Age and called the "Food vessel." This is a peculiarly British type and its origin can be clearly traced to a Neolithic ancestor (11). Neolithic pottery is rare in England, though one or two examples, recalling in shape a proto-type of the Bronze Age "Food vessel," have been dredged from the Thames.

But England was not to be left completely isolated to work out her own salvation. A fresh invasion, this time of a bronze-using people practising cremation, arrived on our shores, and the history of the country passes off the stage set for this little book.

BIBLIOGRAPHY and REFERENCES

(1) L. ARMSTRONG. "Excavations at Mother Grundy's Parlour, Creswell Crags, Derbyshire." *Journ. Roy. Anth. Inst.* vol. LV, Jan.–June, 1925.
(2) See bibliography (5) at end of chapter 1.
(3) R. A. BULLEN. *Harlyn Bay.* Padstow, 1912. A not very complete account with little reference to the earlier Mesolithic industries.
(4) J. B. CALKIN. "Pygmy and other flint implements found at Peacehaven." *Sussex Arch. Coll.* vol. LXV.
(5) W. J. L. ABBOTT. *The Prehistoric Races of Hastings.* Reprinted from *St Paul's Magazine,* 1898.
(6) See bibliography (10) at end of chapter 1.
(7) F. BUCKLEY. "Microlithic industries of Northumberland." *Archaeologia Aeliana,* 4th series, vol. I, 1925. See also *Proceedings of the Soc. Antiq. of Newcastle,* 3rd series, vol. X, 1923.

(8) L. ARMSTRONG. "Two East Yorkshire bone harpoons." *Man*, 1922 (Sept.).

(9) S. H. WARREN. "On the correlation of the Prehistoric 'Floor' at Hullbridge with similar beds elsewhere." *Essex Naturalist*, vol. XVI, 1911.

—— "The classification of the Prehistoric Remains of Eastern Essex." *Journ. Roy. Anth. Inst.* Jan.–June, 1912.

—— "The dating of Surface Flint Implements and the evidences of the Submerged Peat Surface." *Proc. Prehist. Soc. E. Anglia*, vol. III, pt I, 1918–1919.

(10) W. J. KNOWLES. "Report on the Prehistoric Remains from the Sand-hills of the Coast of Ireland." *Proc. Roy. Irish Acad.* Series III, vol. I.

—— " Prehistoric Stone Implements from the River Bann and Lough Neagh." *Proc. Roy. Irish Acad.* vol. XXX, sect. C, No. 7.

G. COFFEY. "The Larne Raised Beach." *Proc. Roy. Irish Acad.* vol. XXV, sect. C, No. 6.

(11) G. W. ABBOTT and R. SMITH. "The Discovery of Prehistoric Pits at Peterborough and the Development of Neolithic Pottery." *Archaeologia*, vol. LXII.

E. T. LEEDS. "Further Discoveries of the Neolithic and Bronze Ages at Peterborough." *Ant. Journ.* vol. II.

(12) A SPECIAL COMMITTEE. "Report of the Excavations at Grimes Graves...." *Prehist. Soc. of E. Anglia*, March–May 1914.

L. ARMSTRONG. See *Proceedings of the Prehist. Soc. of E. Anglia*, vol. III, pt 3; vol. III, pt 4; vol. IV, pt 1; vol. IV, pt 2.

(13) See bibliography (9) at end of chapter II.

(14) O. G. S. CRAWFORD. *The Long Barrows of the Cotswolds.* 1925.

(15) E. H. STONE. *The Stones of Stonehenge.* 1924.

(16) W. D. BUSHELL. "Amongst the Prescelly Circles." *Arch. Cambrensis*, July 1911.

(17) C. Fox. *Archaeology of the Cambridge Region.* 1923.

(18) J. ABERCROMBY. *A Study of the Bronze Age Pottery of Great Britain and Ireland.* 1912.

(19) C. Fox and EARL CAWDOR. "The Beacon Hill Barrow, Barton Mills, Suffolk." *Camb. Antiq. Soc.* vol. XXVI, 1925.

(20) C. Fox. "On two Beakers of the Early Bronze Age...with a record of the distribution of Beaker-pottery in England and Wales." *Cambrian Arch. Assoc.* June 1925.

(21) J. QUINE. "Early Scribed Rocks of the Isle of Man, with notes on the early pottery of the Island." *Camb. Antiq. Soc.* vol. XXIV, 1923.

CHAPTER VIII

THE MEDITERRANEAN AREA AND THE COPPER AGE

I N prehistoric times the Mediterranean area was culturally considerably in advance of the rest of Europe, and it has therefore to be treated separately. While throughout the rest of Europe metal was unknown and only stone was used for tool making, the Mediterranean folk were not only using copper, but in some cases had learnt the hardening effects of the addition of tin, and had begun to manufacture bronze. The use of metal and consequent progress in culture extended right round the central sea; in Spain for example we find copper in full use at a time contemporary with the later developments of the New Stone Age further north. Doubtless this was due in part to the fact that there are large quantities of easily worked copper ore in the country, but there are as well clear indications of influences from the progressive eastern Mediterranean. In spite of the diversity of cultures situated around the central sea this influence engendered a certain unity which runs through the whole.

The Neolithic industries of North Africa, in spite of certain similarities, are not uniform. For example the stone tools found in the Oran are not quite identical with those of the oasis of Siwa and these in turn differ to a certain extent from the industries of the Fayum and Egypt. It seems that from the Capsian (=African Aurignacian) was developed a Mesolithic culture with pigmy tools similar to, if not identical with, the Tardenoisean of Europe. This in turn gave place to a true

Neolithic with small polished stone axes and quantities of little arrow heads. These latter are sometimes leaf-shaped, vaguely recalling in shape Solutrean laurel leaves, sometimes tanged and winged. Now and then small, extremely beautifully made examples are found with their edges denticulated. Pottery was manufactured and was in full use. Exact correlations between these several industries and sub-division into successive cultures have not yet with certainty been determined.

The most important area from the prehistorian's point of view is naturally Egypt(1). The earliest known cultures have been found at Badari (Upper Egypt)[1] and in the Fayum. The latter is probably rather the earlier, though the industries show many common forms. Rough pottery, polished axes, hoes, sickles, knives, and a few bone tools occur in middens, and granaries, consisting of large buried straw baskets, have also been found. The Fayum lake then stood about 200 feet higher than it does to-day, and the Neolithic families lived at the edge. In spite of the time gap, the life of these people must have been not unlike that of the modern desert dweller of the region. At Badari skeletons have been found, but the type seems quite ordinary and slightly negroid.

There follows a succession of industries not easily classed into a "cut and dried" sequence, but the Neolithic Egyptian was certainly a past master in the flaking of flint by a chipping and pressure technique. Late in Neolithic times graves were made

[1] This industry has been claimed to be Solutrean in culture by no less an authority than Professor Flinders Petrie, but his evidence is, to say the least, extremely slender. The occurrence of a quantity of pottery, not to speak of the stone industries themselves, would seem to argue definitely that the culture is Neolithic.

just beyond the cultivated land on the edge of the desert, of which the best known are those of Nakadah, a site some miles to the north of Thebes. The graves often contain a rich funeral furniture and so are of the greatest assistance in obtaining a chronological picture of the life and ideas of these early folk. The body was wrapped in a reed cloth and placed in a wicker box or under an earthenware pot to protect it from being crushed. A flexed position, with the hands up near the face, is usual. The funeral furniture includes pots, the earliest being made of a red polished ware, the tops left black by regulated firing. All sorts of shapes are found, including vases, saucers, etc. Later appears a buff ware, decorated with figures of humans, animals, boats and geometric patterns, including the spiral executed in red paint. Objects of ivory, wood, gold, silver and copper, as well as necklaces of crystal, etc., are found in the graves. Other interesting objects are the so-called palettes made of slate and often cut into the shapes of animal silhouettes; these were perhaps used when tattooing and painting their eyelids. There seem to have been close relations with neighbouring peoples whose influences doubtless helped the rapid progress in culture. Just before the creation of the First Dynasty, when the country was united under one leader, copper was introduced and bronze not long afterwards. Soon after the coming of the Dynasties calligraphy was developed and the story passes out of our purview.

The island of Crete(a) where a maritime race grew up which later had the whole of the sea commerce in its hands is a very important locality. Thick Neolithic deposits have been discovered underlying the Bronze Age palaces at Knossos, and these have yielded well-made pottery, including the well-known "ripple ware," first cousin to a very similar pottery found at Badari. However these Neolithic finds at Knossos do not seem to be very early and are probably later in date than the Badarian discoveries. Cretan Neolithic vases with handles and spouts occur; also steatopygous female figurines of baked clay, these latter connect the culture of the island with the worship of the Great Earth Mother, so widely extended throughout Asia Minor and the Near East generally in very early times[1]. On the north coast of Crete, not far from the modern town of Herakleion, an industry with rough quartzite picks and obsidian flakes and tools (the obsidian probably imported from Melos as it is not found on the island) has been discovered.

The Neolithic industries are succeeded by a rich series of Copper Age or earliest Bronze Age industries called Early Minoan. These are sub-divisible into three periods. In the pottery—sometimes painted with simple geometric patterns—we find various and often grotesque shapes. Long spouts, imitating a bird's beak, the eyes being also in many cases indicated, are of common occurrence. The potter's wheel does not occur till the succeeding full Bronze Age cultures. In the Peloponnese Neolithic pottery has been found near Corinth, smooth, hand-made, and of a greyish colour, apparently undecorated. In some ways the mainland of Greece was less important than the Cycladic Islands, for these latter had rich natural material to export. Thus we find a Parian marble bowl in a First Dynastic tomb in Egypt, while South Russia and Bulgaria, as well as other far distant lands, have yielded objects made from

[1] In this connection the discovery of female figurines in baked clay from very early deposits at Anau III should be noted.

materials only found in the islands. Melos supplied obsidian, Paros marble, Naxos emery, and copper ores occurred both in Paros and Siphnos. But, curiously enough, no very definite Neolithic cultures have been found in the islands themselves. For example, the emery supplied from Naxos to Pre-Dynastic Egypt was apparently collected by prospectors without any considerable habitation of the island even by traders. A little later, at the dawn of the Bronze Age, however, the islands were thickly populated, presumably partly from Asia Minor, partly from Egypt. From now onward the islands came more and more under the influence of the Cretan culture which dominated the Aegean throughout the Bronze Age.

Mesopotamia is still in process of being excavated and much further light on its earliest cultures will no doubt be thrown in the course of the next few years. The Sumerian people, whose origin is unknown, were at one time considered to be the earliest folk in the land, but now painted pottery and other industries of still earlier date have been unearthed at Eridu and many other sites[3]. A glance at chapter III will show that on *a priori* grounds we should expect to look to the southeast, to the now desert wastes of Seistan, for a cradle for the cultures that later sprang into such great prominence between the "rivers"; and in this connection it is interesting to note that lately in the Panjab an industry very similar to that of the Sumerian has been discovered. Whether these two are to be directly connected, or whether they both spring from a common intermediate source is still unknown. We shall refer again to the Sumerian and the cultures immediately succeeding it in the chapter on the Bronze Age, for in this region writing was early invented, and documentary evidence enables us to visualise to some extent what life in the Bronze Age must have been like in these regions.

An important trade centre grew up near the coast of Asia Minor; this was Troy, or Hissarlik as it is often called(4). Many cities, one on top of another, have been unearthed, the sixth from the bottom being the well-known city of Homeric fame. The earliest town, though simple in construction, had stone foundations. A black pottery (the paste being mixed with charcoal), slipped and polished, occurs, occasionally decorated in a simple linear design with white paint. The common form is a bowl of globular shape with eyed lugs for suspension. These are not dissimilar to those found in Crete belonging to the earliest Metal Ages, but there is also a high footed bowl such as is found in Danubian II. Stone celts and a few perforated axes occur, but no metal. The fauna includes sheep, goats, cattle, pigs, and apparently fishing was practised. In the next town, Troy II, which was of considerably greater importance, there were stout walls of stone, $8\frac{1}{2}$ metres high, surmounted by a brick rampart with, as in Mesopotamia, false buttresses at intervals. The houses were of the Megaron type with porch and central hearth; this rather points to a northern influence. This second city of Troy was twice destroyed and rebuilt and can thus be regarded as having had three periods. In the oldest a red pottery was still made by hand, but a little later the wheel appears and also the use of the muffle furnace, which enabled the potter to obtain a black pot by the reduction of the metallic salts contained in the clay. Gold and silver decorated objects occur, but in the latter part of Troy II's existence analysis shows that the advantage of a standard bronze, containing 10 per cent. tin, had been discovered and was in full use; we pass therefore into the Bronze Age. Troy II had a commerce stretching far and wide, and we find connections as far north as the Danube valley.

Following round the Mediterranean(5), we note that South Italy and the island of Sicily yield industries in many ways quite different from those of North Italy and more strongly influenced by the cultures of the eastern Mediterranean; Central and Upper Italy were more connected with the northern European cultures. In South Italy regular villages are found and the burials, sometimes in caves, sometimes in oval trenches, are found near by. The people were long-headed—doubtless survivals of some of the old Upper Capsian stock transformed—and the fauna includes goats, sheep, cattle and swine. The industries, which are not very interesting, include polished stone celts, which are rare, and rough picks made from local rock; the occurrence of obsidian, however, shows that a sea commerce existed, this material not being obtainable locally. Pottery occurs, occasionally painted, but more generally decorated by being impressed, before burning, with an engraved stamp, the incised pattern thus formed being sometimes filled in with a white or, more rarely, red material.

The island of Malta, with its satellite Gozo(6), is of especial interest as a rich culture, starting in Late Neolithic times and persisting during the Bronze Age, was developed there. Elaborate temple buildings were constructed, which on excavation have yielded much pottery including figurines. On the stones of one of these temples a spiral decoration is carved. What appear to be trackways—probably of the same age— have been noted running across the island; there is clear proof that earth movement has depressed the eastern end of the region since they were in use, for in low-lying districts portions of the trackways are to-day under the sea.

Another locality where important cultures were developed is Sardinia, a region rich in obsidian, copper and silver. The earliest industry found there in some respects closely resembles the Maltese, and has been compared with the Early Minoan. Later appeared the true Copper Age of the island when the industries include flat copper celts and bell beakers and show connections with Catalonia and western Europe. The material examined has been largely collected from a great necropolis of chamber graves called Anghelu Ruju.

In Spain very rich Late Neolithic and Copper Age cultures were developed(7), and these are not by any means the same all over the peninsula. To the north, of course, the folk of the Western Area culture supplied a strong influence; but even southwards the industries of the east and centre and west are by no means quite the same.

The old transitional Tardenoisean culture, with the addition of the trapeze and a knowledge of pottery, long survived, and was replaced by an industry with polished stone axes. That the folk of this time were already wealthy is evidenced by the find of a gold diadem in the cave of Los Murciélagos near Albuñol in the province of Granada. Two Copper Age periods followed, each capable of sub-division locally and differing to a certain extent in various parts of the country. The pottery was already well made and the stone industries, including arrow heads and the like, show very considerable skill. In the full Copper Age, or second period, often named Palmella culture, we have

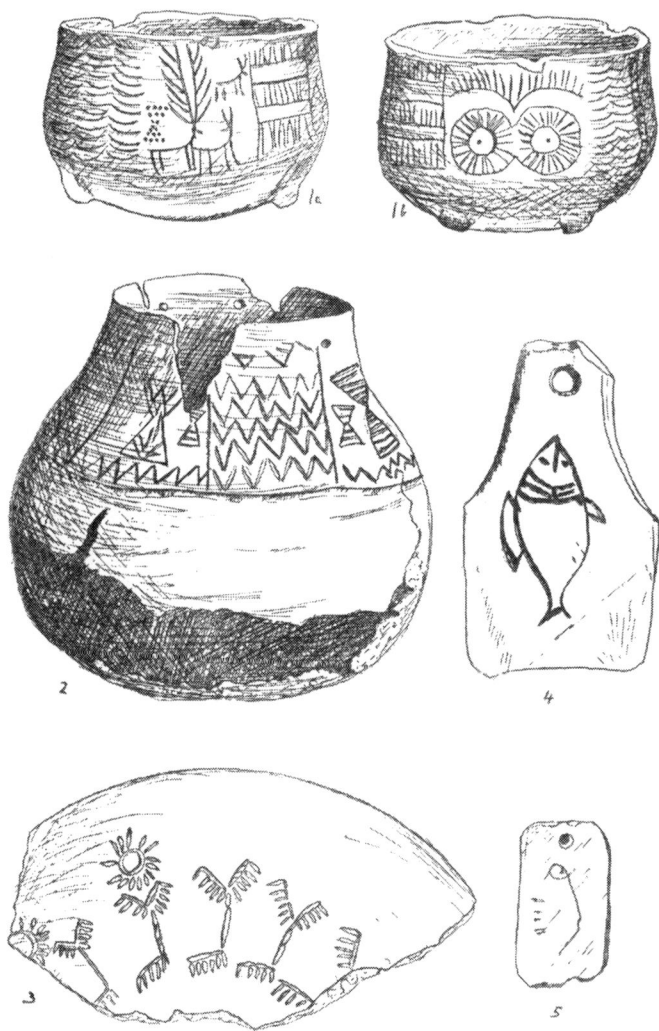

Plate 25. 1, 2, 3. Decorated pottery of Copper Age from Spain.
4, 5. Examples of Neolithic naturalistic art.

well-made pots engraved with figures of convention-
alised stags and human beings (Plate 25, nos. 1, 2, 3).
These correspond closely to the paintings in Spanish
Art Group III described in chapter x. The best-known
sites that have yielded this engraved pottery are Los
Millares and Las Carolinas just south of Madrid near
Ciempozuelos (Plate 25, no. 3).

The tombs of this period are of very considerable
importance(8). Certain peculiar developments that occur
have already been described in chapter vi; there are
also artificial caves, as at Palmella itself, which have
been used as tombs. It is the southern part of the
peninsula with which we are now mostly concerned
and here influences from the eastern Mediterranean
made themselves felt. In the north the types and
developments of megalithic constructions are of the
normal Western Area variety and show clear connections
with France. Thanks to the explorations of Siret,
Obermaier, and a number of Spanish investigators, it
has been found possible to make out a sequence for the
megalithic monuments of the southern area, which
includes parts of South Portugal, as follows:

END OF TRUE NEOLITHIC AGE

At this time we find:

1. Precursors of the true dolmens in the form of
rectangular boxes or circular enclosures. No lid, if
there ever was one, has survived. Little tumulus exists
over the construction.

2. Simple chamber dolmens constructed of rough
flags of a quadrangular or polygonal shape.

In both types are found stone celts with massive
round shafts; ordinary Neolithic flint tools and some
pigmies; points, awls and chisels of bone; simple

pottery (cups and beakers) with a few circles or *pointillé* engraved on them. A few poorly made ornaments such as bored teeth, shells or fragments of bone, etc., occur.

3. Dolmens with small entrances and little covered galleries, their contents being the same as before only of better workmanship. Armlets made from *Pectunculus* shell. The first appearance of a simple form of schist idol.

EARLY COPPER AGE

1. Large passage graves.

2. Big roofed galleries (the latter often of trapezoid shape), their contents being celts frequently made from choice stone; flint arrow heads trimmed over their whole surface, often with tangs and basal wings; large fine dagger blades; pottery with rich linear decoration —geometric pattern, wavy lines or spirals, etc.—the first appearance of bell beakers; beads of callais; schist idols; amulets of animal phalanges. In the south of the peninsula copper now appears for the first time.

FULL COPPER AGE

(Two zones—one in the south; the other in the north.) In the south or rather south-west zone we find:

1. Cupola dolmens with or without entrance galleries or interior annexes.

2. Ordinary dolmens with entrances and covered galleries.

At the beginning of this time the change in building referred to in chapter VI appears. Formerly, as has been said, the uprights of the chamber and gallery supported the roof, but now the excavation method is employed. Locally, however, the simple passage grave with the old technique continues to exist.

The contents of the dolmens are similar to those last enumerated. Besides these we find well-made little votive celts; fine daggers and blades of flint; arrow heads, some with long tangs and tail-like basal wings, either willow or reed shaped; bone beads and round-eyed needles; tools and weapons of copper—flat axes and blades; pottery of the Ciempozuelos type with bell-beakers, the decoration purely geometric or figurative—sun pictures, conventionalised animals, eye ornaments, etc. (Plate 25, nos. 1–3). Painted vessels are rare. We also find beads, etc., of gold, silver, copper, gilded lead, ivory, amber, amethyst, turquoise, callais; armlets of ivory or thin stone plates; palettes; ointment jars; human-shaped flat idols of stone; schist idols, often with rich engravings of rough representations of humans—frequently painted; cone-shaped idols of alabaster, lime-stone, etc.; idols made from phalange bones, often richly painted or engraved.

In the north zone we find:

1. Short passage graves.

2. Kist-shaped chambers.

The contents are more or less similar to those of the last list, the finely worked flint arrow heads, sometimes tanged and with basal wings, sometimes leaf-shaped, being specially numerous. There are fairly rich copper finds; pottery slightly decorated with patterns of Ciem-pozuelos type; bell beakers; beads of stone and mussel shell; small ornaments of gold, silver, copper, amber. Rare examples of trephining have been noted.

EARLY BRONZE AGE

In this we find small stone kists with covering lids. The contents of the kists show a falling off in the flint industry, but are rich in copper tools along with which bronze becomes more frequent. We find awls, chisels, thin flat axes with curved edges, sword blades and triangular daggers, rings and armlets. Also plain matt pottery of the El Argar type, as well as square-shaped bone beads and ornaments of gold, silver and amber.

The finding of beakers in Spain at such a very early date is naturally of first-class importance, and it is believed that the peninsula was actually the cradle of this mysterious and elusive people. Their subsequent wanderings carried them and their pots over most of Europe and as far east as Hungary. They spread north-wards to Brittany and perhaps via the pass of Belfort down the Rhine to our own country. They crossed to Italy and probably attained Central Europe via the Brenner Pass. Naturally some modifications in pot type, etc., occur in different districts; thus the pots at Carnac are not quite the same as those of England, and in Bohemia(?) handled cups develop, these in turn being distributed over an area far outside their original home. The Beaker folk were round-headed and burials were by inhumation.

Spain was doubtless very important to the progressive eastern Mediterranean cultures from its having metal ores, and it is surprising to note the failure of this brilliant cradle of culture to develop further. The early Bronze Age (El Argar) culture proved to be of some importance and spread to Italy, but from that time onwards Spain for long ceased to count. One is tempted to wonder whether the hardy and by now skilful mariner from Crete may not have penetrated even beyond Spain, and whether we should not look to him as the cause of the great developments that took place in South Brittany in Early Metal Age times? Although the cultures found at Carnac point to a limited use of metal, there is no reason to consider that the date is anything far anterior to that of the Early Bronze Age in Crete; the occurrence of tin ores in Brittany, not to speak of callais and other products, might well tempt the Mediterranean merchant. Much has been written by some authors of the influence of Phoenician traders in very early times; it may be that further discoveries will substitute the word Cretan for Phoenician in the prehistoric periods at the dawn of the Metal Age in northern Europe.

Should the above really represent a true state of affairs then the anomalous and splendid development of culture in the south of Brittany—especially near Carnac —becomes explicable, and as it would have owed its origin to the Mediterranean influence this is the place to give a brief description of it rather than when the Neolithic of the Western Area was under review. French prehistorians have long classed the finds at Carnac as Late Neolithic, but metal has been found and the Age is really Copper or Early Bronze. The modern village of Carnac lies some two or three miles from the sea in sight of the long peninsula of Quiberon. The surrounding district is poor, from an agricultural point of view, and there is but little depth of soil. But what it lacks in fertility is made up in the interest of its prehistoric remains, and the whole country-side must have been a sacred area, being more than rich in menhirs, cromlechs, alignments, dolmens, and other complicated megalithic tombs. To the eastward lies the shallow Morbihan Sea full of islands, and there is direct evidence of land submergence since "Carnacian" times, there being several menhirs and cromlechs that are now no longer above high-water level. The menhirs are of the usual kinds and are often of immense size. The alignments are world-famous and have been described in chapter VI. It is interesting to note that the alignments at Carnac cross, without regard, over an earlier burial marked by a menhir which is out of line with the smaller menhirs forming the main alignment. Such a definite sequence is important though naturally it does not indicate that all single menhirs are necessarily early. Cromlechs and dolmens are of the usual type and much in the way of funeral furniture has been recovered in spite of the fact that a large number of the monuments had been long known and pillaged. Owing to the scarcity of soil the artificial earth mounds previously covering the tombs were of great importance to agriculturists. Simple and complicated passage graves occur —the most famous being that of St Michel, near the modern village of Carnac overlooking the alignments of Menec, where there is a complicated series of chambers and passages. Apparently a person of great importance was buried here with perhaps his servants and oxen. Some metal was also discovered therein. Many of these megalithic buildings have rough carvings on them. These include serpents—said to be drawn in connection with polished celts, a conventional octopus(?) looking in reality rather like a shield, so-called waving corn, etc. In one instance, in a tomb at Gavr'inis, an island in the Morbihan Sea, there is a design closely resembling that on a tumulus grave at Sess Kilgreen in Ireland. Probably Gavr'inis was actually an Irish colony in Brittany. Among the natural products of South Brittany is a very fine bluish-green serpentine rock and finely polished celts of a very late type are found far and wide made from this material; which seems to have been a favourite article of commerce, though not rivalling the well-known honey-coloured flint of Grand Pressigny. Two such celts have been found for example near Cambridge.

But it was not only through Spain that the progressive cultures of the eastern Mediterranean reached northern Europe. Direct intercourse between Cyprus and Troy on the one hand and Hungary on the other is proved by the finding of southern types of tools in the north. This commerce seems further to have introduced the copper worker of Hungary to the tin producer of Bohemia, and the result was naturally fertile in progress. The bell beaker folk added their quota and there arose in these lands the so-called Marschwitz culture with its handled cups, etc. that just preceded the true Bronze Age. Flat graves containing contracted bodies occur and the funeral furniture includes eastern types of battle axes.

BIBLIOGRAPHY and REFERENCES

(1) E. A. W. BUDGE. *Egypt.* (Home University Series.)
(2) H. R. HALL. *Aegean Archaeology.* 1914.
(3) H. R. HALL. "The Excavations of 1919...." *Man,* 1925, 1. See also V. G. Childe, *The Most Ancient East.* 1928.
(4) DÖRPFELD. *Troja und Ilios.* 1902.
(5) See bibliography (1) at end of chapter v.
(6) M. A. MURRAY. *Excavations in Malta.* 1923. Miss Murray gives a number of plates illustrating her finds and the whole forms a convenient volume. Most of the excavation in Malta, however, and its subsequent publication is due to the labours of Professor T. Zammit.
(7) N. ÅBERG. *La Civilisation Énéolithique dans la Péninsule Ibérique.* 1921.
(8) H. OBERMAIER. "Die Dolmen Spaniens." *Mitt. d. Anth. Gesellsch. in Wien,* Band L, 1920.

CHAPTER IX

PRELIMINARY NOTES ON THE BRONZE AGE CULTURES

Bronze is an alloy of copper and tin. True bronze contains 10 per cent. of the latter metal and is a harder and tougher material than copper itself and therefore more useful for the purpose of tool and weapon making.

No hard and fast line can be drawn between the Copper and Bronze cultures of Europe; the alloy was not introduced by invading warriors from outside, but appears as an autochthonous development. That copper could be hardened by the addition of other metals— tin, antimony, etc.—had already been discovered in the Copper Age and apparently many experiments were tried before standard bronze was evolved. Cultural developments were not uniform all over Europe and it is near tin producing areas—tin ores are rarer than those of copper—that the earliest true Bronze Age industries develop. As formerly, however, the eastern Mediterranean area was the most progressive and the use of bronze started earlier there than in northern Europe, the necessary tin being obtained through an extensive commerce, which incidentally introduced many objects from the Aegean into the northern lands and helped to forward the new culture there.

The Bronze Age can be divided into four periods, the earliest being called Bronze I and the latest Bronze IV. In some districts, e.g. East Anglia, only two periods can be clearly demonstrated; the sharp dividing line is always between Bronze IV and the earlier periods[1]. The periods are demonstrated partly on stratigraphical, but largely on typological grounds, the evolution of various tools being determined. An outline study of the development of some of the more important implements[1] will therefore be necessary before proceeding further, stress naturally being laid on types belonging to the earlier periods, as Bronze IV is really outside the purview of this book[2].

CELTS

One of the commonest tool families is that of the Celt. It commences in the Copper Age and its evolution can be seen by reference to Plate 26, nos. 1–9. At first the shape is that of a simple chisel—usually made of copper—and the tool is clearly derived from the stone celt. Next side ridges appear, doubtless to keep the tool in place when hafted, and in this connection there also grows a transverse ridge, called a stop ridge, which prevents the haft being pushed down too far. Thus there develops the so-called "Palstave"[2] (Plate 26, no. 5). But side by side with this there was evolved the winged type, where the side ridges increase to such an extent that they bend over and meet. At first the wings appear at the middle of the celt, later at the butt end (Plate 26, nos. 6 and 7). The winged type is a continental development and from it the

[1] Chance finds of bronze tools occur, especially near such places as convenient fords where trackways converged. Implements are found too in burials and also form hoards—these being formerly the "capital" of an individual or the stock in trade of a merchant. The so-called Wilburton hoard—preserved to-day in the Cambridge Museum of Archaeology and Ethnology—may be taken as an example. Apparently it was being transported across a mere when the boat capsized: the tools were preserved in the peat below.

[2] Side rings for attachment purposes are often found in several types of celt.

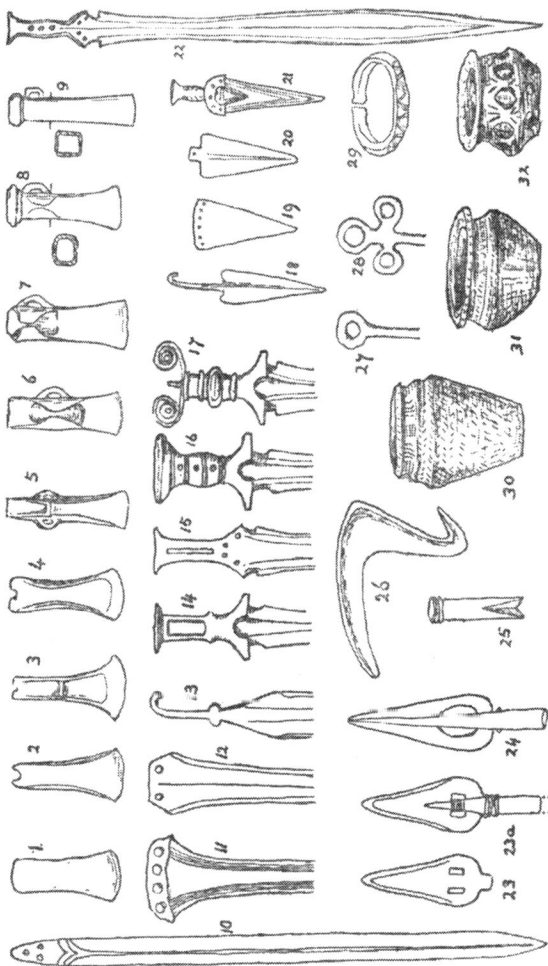

Plate 26. Examples illustrating the principal types of Bronze Age tools. 1–9 show the evolution of the celt during the Bronze Age.

socketed celt was derived by the complete closing of the wings and suppression of the central septum. Sometimes an idea of the wings persists as an art motif engraved round the socket (Plate 26, no. 8). The socketed celt only occurs in Bronze IV, a statement applicable to most of the socketed types of tools which are seldom found earlier than the end of the Bronze III period. The evolution of the celt can be tabulated as follows:

1. Flat celts   ...   .   Bronze I
2. Slightly raised edges   ...   .   Bronze II
3. Stop ridges   ...   .   Bronze II
4. Much raised edges   ...   .   Bronze III
5. Palstaves   ...   .   Bronze III and Early IV
6. (a) Wings at middle of celt ...   ...   Bronze III
   (b) Wings at butt end of celt...   ...   Bronze III and Early IV
7. Socketed celts:
   (a) Round socket hole   ...   ...   Bronze IV
   (b) Square or oblong socket hole ...   Bronze IV

DAGGERS

Only in period Bronze I and II are the types of daggers at all distinctive. There are three varieties as follows: (a) Triangular shaped with a large base, the blade being flat or ridged centrally on both faces to ensure strength. There are rivet holes for attachment to hafts but neither tongue nor tang, except very rudimentarily (Plate 26, no. 19). This variety is found in Copper Age industries and during Bronze I and II periods. (b) Similar to (a) but with a distinct tongue (Plate 26, no. 20). This variety is found too in the same industries. (c) Slender and with a long tang, which, especially in the eastern Mediterranean area, is often turned over at the end. There is a central ridge to ensure strength to the long narrow blade (Plate 26, no. 18). This variety is called *Cypriote* and it occurs at the end of the Bronze I period[1].

RAPIERS AND SWORDS

There are many varieties of these, two of which are derived from dagger prototypes, i.e. from the triangular dagger (Plate 26, nos. 11 and 12); and the Cypriote dagger (Plate 26, nos. 10 and 13). A third variety has no dagger prototype, but the blades are leaf-shaped and the handles are varied and complicated (Plate 26, nos. 14, 15, 16, 17, 22). The first two varieties are mostly to be dated to Bronze II or III periods, occasionally to the end of Bronze I while the third is typical of the Bronze IV period.

LANCES

Of these there are two varieties. The one called the Amorgos lance has a flat blade with tongue and methods for attachment to a haft, and occurs at the end of the Bronze I and during the Bronze II periods (Plate 26, no. 23; 23*a* shows ditto hafted). The other is a socketed variety, there being several means of firmly affixing a haft which gave rise to numerous different types. The socketed lance does appear very occasionally as early as the end of Bronze II, but is rare before the end of Bronze III and Bronze IV periods (Plate 26, no. 24).

ARROW HEADS

Although bronze arrow heads occur, flint continued to be used in most districts for arrow head making till the Bronze IV period and it is not easy to say whether any given arrow head, found on the surface without

[1] Several specimens were found in the second city of Troy which can be correlated with the last phases of the Early Minoan culture in Crete.

datable associated objects, is of Neolithic or Bronze Age. As a rule the later examples are better made and it has been suggested that the basal wings are more parallel, whereas in the case of Neolithic examples they tend to be divergent.

PINS

Types of pins vary considerably during the Bronze Age and some of them are also especially characteristic of certain areas. Thus the examples figured on Plate 26, nos. 27 and 28, belong to the Aunjetitz culture, which is the earliest Bronze culture in the north and is especially centred in the districts now known as Bohemia. In France pins are rare before the Late Bronze Age.

There are many other kinds of Bronze articles, such as gouges (Plate 26, no. 25), knives, sickles (Plate 26, no. 26), bracelets (Plate 26, no. 29), buttons, armour, harness and the like. But these are perhaps of less importance for our purpose and those desiring a detailed study of them must consult works specially devoted to the Bronze Age. Sandstone moulds for making all the foregoing tools have been found.

POTTERY

There is considerable variety in the pottery, both in the shapes and decorations; also many modifications in different localities. In England three important types, usually associated with burials, can be noted(3): (a) the "cinerary urn" (Plate 26, no. 30), (b) the "food vessel" (Plate 26, no. 31), and (c) the "incense cup" (Plate 26, no. 32).

TRADE ROUTES

Although districts bordering the eastern Mediterranean were far more progressive than regions further

north, trade routes sprang up in Early Bronze times
and an interchange of culture developed. The chief
article of commerce seems to have been amber, the
Baltic variety being especially prized by the dwellers
in the south. The trade routes followed as far as possible river valleys and spread from Jutland up the valley
of the Elbe and thence through Bohemia and along
the Moldau over to the valley of the Inn. Italy was
reached by the Brenner Pass, which being under 5000
feet in height was already open in Copper Age times(4).
There was a second main route from the eastern Baltic
to Italy via Styria, but it was only opened in Early Iron
Age, i.e. Hallstatt times. The trade routes and their
use by folk of the various periods is demonstrated by
observing industries of a given period, restricted to
narrow belts following the courses of suitable rivers
and converging on possible passes.

HABITATIONS

Two kinds of Bronze Age village are known—lake
dwellings and land habitations. The former were
exactly like the Neolithic prototypes, except that they
were usually built further out in the lakes. The latter
were ordinary primitive villages with narrow streets
often surrounded with a well-built mortarless wall.
A variety is however known where the villages were
built on piles over dry land. They are known as *Terre-
mare* settlements(5).

BURIALS

It is often said that cremation first appeared with
the Bronze Age cultures. This is not strictly true for
cremation has been observed occurring sporadically as
early as Neolithic times. However in the Bronze IV

period cremation becomes the usual mode for disposal of the dead, the ashes being either placed in a pot and buried under a round tumulus or collected into a small scooped out hollow in the ground under the mound. Many causes may have led to the rise of cremation. Probably practical reasons underlay its use at first— elimination of infection in cases of epidemics among a by now numerous population, etc.; later doubtless religion became involved in the custom and a ritual interpretation was evolved. Frequently a necropolis is formed by the grouping together of Bronze Age tumulus graves and such a necropolis is of especial importance to the student as the graves generally contain a rich funeral furniture. Three of these grave fields are to be noted in connection with the study of the earlier periods. The one is at Aunjetitz in Bohemia[6] and has given much information about the earliest Bronze Age north of the Alps, the others at Remedello and Fontanella (Brescia) lie south of the mountains in North Italy[7].

AEGEAN AREA

As before, the most brilliant cultures were developed in the Mediterranean area and those of the island of Crete are in some ways to us the most startling[8]. Here have been dug up not only whole Bronze Age towns with their narrow paved streets just wide enough for a pack-horse and clearly not meant for wheeled traffic, for regular steps were formed where the road became too steep, but also great palaces once occupied by wealthy king-priests. These palaces are not only richly decorated with frescoes and the like, but have yielded wonderful coloured faience figures and other objects from their magazines and treasuries. Nor is it only from the point of view of beauty and decoration that we are astonished, for we even find baths and a completely furnished drainage system. One of the things that struck the writer most when he visited Knossos was a flight of steps at the back of the palace leading down towards the river. The steps turned at the bottom, and by their side ran a gutter to carry water into a settling tank whence it was conveyed into a cistern, fresh water being a valuable commodity. The gutter, if it had run straight down and then turned at right angles would have been useless and the water would have flooded over the steps and been lost. The gutter was therefore shaped into a series of parabolic curves, so that there was no rush of water and it flowed quietly into the settling tank.

The Bronze cultures of the island are called Minoan and have been divided by Sir Arthur Evans into three periods, each period being in turn sub-divided into three. We thus speak of an Early Minoan 1, 2, 3, Middle Minoan 1, 2, 3, and a Late Minoan 1, 2, 3[1]. The pottery shows influences both from Egypt and Asia Minor. It was often extremely beautifully made and decorated, generally speaking the fashion being dark paint on a light ground in the Early Minoan, light on dark in the Middle Minoan, and again dark on light in the Late Minoan times.

In the Late Bronze Age or Late Minoan times the culture spread to the mainland of Greece and there gave rise to the splendid Mycenean culture, described, at a much later date, by Homer. But Greece had its own Bronze Age cultures long before this Cretan invasion;

---

[1] A comparative dating of Cretan with Egyptian cultures is obtained by the finding of datable Egyptian objects in the various Cretan industries and *vice versa*.

they are called Helladic(9). At first only a simple hand-made, yellow-coloured, generally undecorated pottery was manufactured, but in Middle Helladic times a matt-painting technique developed, and this coincides with the appearance of a bluish-coloured, undecorated ware with a soapy feel called Minyan; it perhaps indicates connections with Asia Minor. That Asia Minor played a part in the development of Bronze Age culture in Greece is further shown by the finding in an early chamber tomb at Mycenae of a seal engraved with symbols clearly from Asia Minor. The Middle Helladic culture was swept away with the coming of the Cretans.

If a European of 150 years ago could have been introduced into the Bronze Age world—especially into the Aegean regions—he would probably soon have been able to adapt himself to the prevailing conditions of life. Even in the north he would not lack for such a small matter as clothes. A sort of woven dressing-gown-like garment has actually been recovered in Denmark perfectly preserved in the peat. In Egypt and Mesopotamia documentary evidence early helps us to fill in the life picture. Mesopotamia(10) especially is proving of interest for, unlike Egypt, it was never a naturally isolated area. Of the earliest Mesopotamians we know little, except that a well-burnt painted ware was manufactured. But with the arrival of the Sumerians, writing on clay tablets commenced. These people were cradled to the east-wards—possibly in the then more fertile, but to-day desert, regions of Seistan and Baluchistan[1]. They were a bureaucratic, business-like folk living in city kingdoms. They had powers of organisation as is shown by the temple records. The temple was the centre of the city,

---

[1] A nearly related culture—possibly derived from the same centre —has lately been found in the north of India.

being both church and government offices while the king was also the chief priest. Fusion of the Sumerians with a Semitic people lying to the north introduced a new outlook on life and to this period must be dated the growth of legends about the creation of the world, a great flood, etc.—legends which at a later date were drawn upon by the Jewish priesthood after the "Captivity" for the writing of their more spiritualised account of the origin and early history of humanity.

Railways, motor cars and wireless were not yet invented, but in many ways it was all very modern. Man had indeed not yet harnessed nature and forced her to do his work for him—doubtless therefore unemployment was less rife!—but, though primitive, life was essentially modern in organisation. The domain of the prehistorian is over.

BIBLIOGRAPHY AND REFERENCES

(1) C. Fox. *The Archaeology of the Cambridge Region.* 1923.
(2) J. Déchelette. *Manuel d'Archéologie....* Tome II, 1910; and H. Peake. *The Bronze Age and the Celtic World.* 1922.
(3) See bibliography (18) at end of chapter VII.
(4) J. M. de Navarro. "Prehistoric Routes between Northern Europe and Italy defined by the Amber Trade." *Geographical Journal,* December 1925.
(5) T. E. Peet. *The Stone and Bronze Ages in Italy.* 1909.
(6) J. Schránil. *Studie o vzniku cultury bronzové v Čechách.* (French résumé.) Prague, 1921.
(7) See *Bullettino di Paletnologia Italiana,* x and xxiv. Also T. E. Peet, *ibid.*
(8) See bibliography (2) at the end of chapter VIII.
(9) C. W. Blegen. "Korakou," *American School of Classical Studies at Athens.* 1921.
(10) H. R. Hall. *The Ancient History of the Near East.* 5th ed. 1920. J. H. Breasted. *Ancient Times....* 1916.

CHAPTER X

ART

A STUDY of the art of a people is always of particular interest whether the art is intended for utilitarian purposes, as was the case with Upper Palaeolithic man, or whether we are dealing with art for art's sake, as seems to have been the case in later prehistoric times. A great deal of the archaeologist's work consists of excavating the dust bins of the prehistoric folk, and we are apt to think only in terms of the kitchen. Art introduces us to some of the higher emotions of the people and gives us a glimpse at their thoughts and feelings. Art decoration is incidentally extremely important to the prehistorian when tracing out connections of cultures and movements of peoples. Art technique and designs are as a rule far more specialised than any tool—even more specialised than the form of a pot or its handle. The occurrence of two objects similar in design and decoration in widely separated areas proves a connection between the areas, either racially or commercially.

MESOLITHIC ART

But little in the way of Mesolithic art existed or has survived to-day. That of Azilian culture as well as that from the Maglemosean and Kitchen Midden sites has already been noted. So far no Tardenoisean or Asturian art has been recognised. An art-group of rock engravings (Plate 28, Fig. 2) is, however, known, occurring in sites along the coast of Norway as far north as Narvik, but only spreading eastwards into Sweden at one place near

Trondhjem where passage of the hills is practicable and easy(1). The date of this group of rock engravings appears to be the full Neolithic Age, for at one site at Bardal, near Trondhjem, examples are found engraved on rocks that, according to Scandinavian geologists, form a terrace that was below sea level until Passage Grave times. Again, at the same site engravings belonging to this group are found underneath other engravings belonging to a much later art-group of the full Bronze Age, thousands of examples of which are found further south in Bohuslain, just north of Gothenburg. Although the Norwegian group cannot be earlier in time than the Passage Grave Period, yet the fact that the figures are often drawn in a naturalistic, or at any rate semi-naturalistic manner, suggests that they were made by folk belonging to the Arctic culture which, it will be remembered, was probably derived directly from the Maglemosean culture of Mesolithic times, but which survived and continued to develop on its own lines in areas not occupied by the Neolithic civilisation that took its place around the shores of the Baltic.

The Norwegian group of drawings includes both engravings and paintings, although the former are by far the most numerous. The engraved figures are generally found carved on extraordinarily hard glacier-worn rocks which turn the blade of a knife to-day; presumably the engravings were elaborately pecked out with a pointed stone chisel. The animals figured include a beautifully drawn reindeer at Böla and others at Bögge, at the end of the Langfjord and elsewhere. An engraving of a fish occurs at another site further north. The animals are often poorly drawn, but this is not to be wondered at considering how extraordinarily refractory the hard rock is. Sometimes only two legs are figured, sometimes four, but even in the latter case there is no attempt at perspective. Often a peculiar method is employed and the lines representing the legs are produced till they meet the line of the back. Only one or two instances of painting are known, which is not surprising as paint cannot sink into these hard rock surfaces and is therefore liable to suffer damage from weathering action, although, on the other hand, it is saved from the dangers which attend the disintegration of rock surfaces due to the action of lichens and other rock-growing plants. A good example of paintings of this group can be seen in a small rock shelter which is situated almost opposite where the road coming over from the head of Langfjord meets the Sundalsfjord. The paintings are in red and represent reindeer, etc., but are not very well drawn. Further north at a site called Leka some little conventionalised human figures, also painted in red, have been observed.

Attempts have been made to connect this art with that of the Laplanders, but though perhaps it is not fair to compare art techniques when used on such different surfaces as rock and bone, it can safely be said that the Lap technique, as seen in the engravings on pieces of bone, etc., has little in common with that of the Norwegian group that we have been describing.

No similar finds elsewhere have been recorded and it would seem likely that we are dealing with an isolated manifestation of art made by folk belonging to the Arctic culture; why and for what purpose they were made is completely unknown. At a later time Bronze Age folk inhabited the district, at any rate around Trondhjem, and at Bardal the art of these new people is found superimposed on examples of the older group. Probably

the Arctic culture people became extinct or were absorbed by the new comers, unless it should prove that
some distant connection between them and the Laps of
to-day can be clearly determined.

NEOLITHIC AND EARLIEST METAL AGE ART

Two groups can be distinguished in the Neolithic
and Copper Age art: the first comprises decorated
objects, such as pots or tools, etc., and the second
drawings on rocks or in rock shelters which are, however, of rare occurrence. The first of these groups has
been largely discussed in chapter IV, and it is only
necessary here to remind readers of the extremely fine
and well-drawn patterns on the beautifully made pots
of Early Neolithic date in the Eastern Area, or, again,
of the elaborate decoration on the collar flasks of
Scandinavia, not to speak of the complicated and extremely decorative motifs found at the end of Neolithic
times for them to realise that Neolithic man was not
in the least devoid of artistic sense. Prehistorians are
rather apt, after studying the wonderful cave art of
Upper Palaeolithic man, to underrate the powers and
the artistic appreciation of his Neolithic successor, but
this is largely due to the fact that the Neolithic decoration of pots consisted exclusively, or almost exclusively,
of finely drawn geometric patterns. Naturalistic drawings of animals were not employed as motifs, as on the
rounded surface of a pot they would not only have been
exceedingly difficult to execute, but also not particularly
adaptable. In the Mediterranean area, at that time
always far in advance of northern Europe in culture,
it was not till Late Minoan (Bronze) times that plants
and other natural objects were employed as motifs for
decoration.

One or two chipped pieces of rock marked with rough geometric patterns have been found at the stone factory site at Penmaenmawr in North Wales. That Neolithic man was not incapable of drawing a naturalistic figure of an animal when he wanted, can be seen in the drawing of a fish on a cork float(2) found by the Lake of Lucerne, figured in Plate 25, no. 4; and a fish, though very poorly executed, can be recognised engraved on a polished piece of greenstone now in the Museum at Carnac, Brittany (Plate 25, no. 5).

Neolithic man was also capable of painting his pots before firing so that the paint cannot be removed by friction or washing. Although this painting decoration, as far as Europe is concerned, is only found in certain circumscribed localities at the very end of Neolithic or rather at the dawn of the Copper Age, it was probably practised in the very earliest times, for we find painted pottery in the earliest levels at Anau in Russian Turkestan, and Neolithic painted pottery has been described from the loess in China. Although the folk who made the wonderful painted pots found in the bottom layers at Susa(3), as well as the people of Abu Shahrein (=Eridu, Mesopotamia) and other places who have left us examples of their workmanship, probably of Pre-Sumerian times(4), knew about the use of metal, it must be remembered that in these areas by the great rivers Euphrates and Tigris the use of metal dates back to extremely early times, far earlier than was the case in northern Europe; and, on the other hand, little is known as to an earlier true Neolithic stage of culture in these regions. In Moravia, at the end of Neolithic times, a painted pottery was developed, but in this case the paint was not fired with the pot and can be removed by friction. The oft mentioned pottery figurines of humans and animals are naturally of great importance (Plates 20, 21 and 29, no. 5). Bronze Age pottery continued to be decorated with incised geometric patterns and painting developed to a high degree in the Aegean area. Even metal tools are sometimes found decorated with zigzag or lozenge patterns.

ROCK SHELTER ART

An extremely interesting art-group that occurs in rock shelters belonging to the Late Neolithic and Copper Age periods has been studied in the Spanish Peninsula(s). Although it occurs sporadically over a great part of South Spain where natural rock shelters in limestone or sandstone occur and conditions are favourable, it can be more or less grouped into distinct areas. The first of these areas is in the extreme south-west of Spain, and is the tract of country bounded by the sea coast and an artificial line drawn from Malaga to Seville and Cadiz. The examples are especially numerous around the Laguna de la Janda where a few years ago M. Breuil and the writer explored nearly sixty sites. Another area is in Murcia and Almeria, South-East Spain, with a focus at Velez Blanco, a little village some sixty miles or so west of Murcia. Here examples of this Copper Age art (often called Spanish Art Group III) come in contact with a naturalistic group (Spanish Art Group II) probably dating back to Quaternary times and contemporary with, though different in technique from the well-known Upper Palaeolithic cave paintings of France or Spain. It is interesting to note, as a proof of the relative ages, that where examples of these two groups, easily differentiated by their vastly different techniques, are found in one and the same rock shelter, if superposition occurs examples of Spanish

Art Group III are invariably painted over and are therefore younger than examples of Spanish Art Group II.
Painted rock shelters have been discovered in the Sierra
Morena, and in the chains of mountains that connect it
with the high land of South-East Portugal. An analogous
art has been found in some rock shelters in the well-
known valley of Las Batuecas(6), mentioned by Borrow
in his *Bible in Spain* as being a mysterious and dreaded
place, though whether this was due to its lonely position
or to legends and traditions dating as far back as Copper
Age times when the paintings were being made, cannot
of course be determined. Las Batuecas lies to the south-
west of Salamanca. In North Spain few examples of
Copper Age paintings have been recognised, with the
exception of an anomalous find at Peña Tú, to be
described later.

This art-group, as a whole, is highly conventionalised
and especially noteworthy for the large number of
geometric patterns, including in one instance the spiral,
and the variety of conventionalisations of the human
form. Some of these are figured in Plate 30; they are
important as they help to show the connection between
the interesting Copper Age culture of the southern
Spanish Peninsula with that of regions elsewhere.
Besides conventionalised human beings, a number of
still more conventionalised animals can be recognised,
including stag, hind, ibex and carnivorous animals
whose species it is difficult to determine. At Las Figuras
near the Laguna de la Janda a large number of birds
are also figured, but, with the exception of one example
in a rock shelter in the Sierra Morena, they do not
appear in the drawings elsewhere. At the same site
is portrayed the figure of a man having in his hand what
seems from its shape to be a metal axe, but on the other

hand at Los Molinos, a site near Velez Blanco, there is
another example portraying equally clearly a stone axe,
and examples of this can be duplicated from Bacinete,
a site not far from Los Barrios in the region of Gibraltar.
At the rock shelter of Los Letreros (Velez Blanco)
a man is figured carrying a sickle in each hand. Judging
by their size, relative to the human figure, they would
seem to be wooden sickles hafted with flints, and not
metal sickles, which, owing to the value of the metal,
were always relatively very small in the Early Metal
Ages. That the folk who made these paintings practised
the domestication of animals is shown by a very charm-
ing example found at Las Canforras de Penarrubia in
the Sierra Morena of an animal being led by a halter.
In the district to the west of the Sierra Morena, lying
between it and Portugal, can be seen some very interesting paintings of wheeled vehicles(7). The paintings
consist of two more or less converging lines with cross-
bars between them, and these converging lines, after
joining, are continued as one line indicating the central
shaft of the vehicle. Two or sometimes four wheels
are indicated by round circles placed just outside these
lines. It is as if the vehicle had been laid out flat, with
the wheels spread on the ground, and was viewed from
above. Exactly the same type of farm cart can be seen
used by the peasants in parts of Spain to-day. The
wheels depicted usually show four spokes, forming
two diameters of the circle at right angles; but in one
instance they are formed by one diameter to the wheel
and two chords at right angles to this diameter, thus
dividing the wheel into three sections (Plate 27, no. 3).
A somewhat similar type of spoking is still used to-day.
At Las Batuecas (Estramadura)(6) the art is not quite
analogous to that further south, and more than one

series of different ages can be determined by a study of their superposition. The lowest is considerably more naturalistic and it may be that this is earlier in date than the art we have been discussing, being possibly true Neolithic or even Azilian. Drawings of comb-shaped figures can be matched with similar finds in the south-west of Spain and are common in the latest examples of art at La Pileta cave near Rhonda(8). The anomalous example of Peña Tú already mentioned is extremely important(9). If the student alights at the little station of Vidiago on the narrow gauge railway from Santander to Llanes (Asturias), he will find, on looking westward, that the sea shore is close by on his right hand, while on his left the ground rises rapidly forming a first foot-hill of the Picos de Europa massif. On the top of this first ridge is a large and very visible block of rock standing up rather like a small Dartmoor tor. On one side it is heavily undercut by natural action, and it is here that the paintings have been preserved. They consist of innumerable red dots, a few very poorly made animal figures, some simple conventional-ised human forms, and a sword, evidently metal, deeply engraved, with five rivet holes near the handle shown in red; there is also a large coffin-shaped idol, partly painted, partly also deeply engraved, this is best de-scribed by reference to Plate 27, no. 1. Peña Tú is the only site in this group where engraving has been em-ployed in conjunction with painting, and it forms a link with the punctuations, the poorly drawn animals and the conventionalised human beings of the regular Spanish Art Group III art on the one hand, and with the carved and painted schist idols in the funeral furniture of the megalithic tombs on the other. The presence of the long triangular sword or dagger indicates an Early

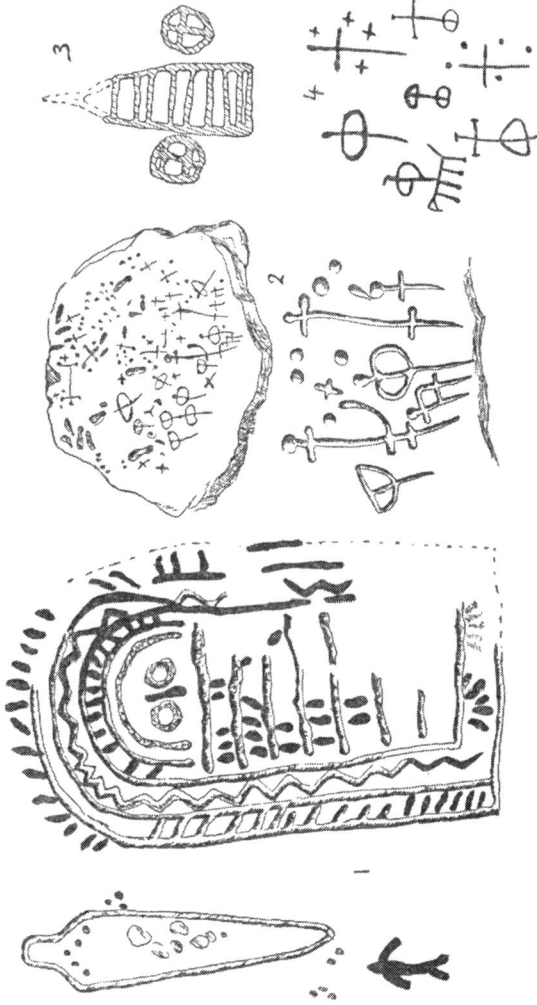

Plate 27. 1. Rock shelter art at Peña Tú (Spain). 2. Rock carving at Clonfinlough (Ireland). 3. Painting of a wheeled cart from the Spanish Art Group III. 4. Rock carvings similar to 2 but from Galicia (Spain).

Metal Age. In North-West Spain Dr Obermaier has studied in the province of Galicia a series of rock carvings(10). These are deeply cut on hard rocks and can be divided into an older and newer series. Although Dr Obermaier suggests a Bronze Age for both series it may be possible to date the earlier as belonging to the Copper Age culture. Figures of the human form conventionalised as well as other geometric figures occur and though not exactly similar would appear to have relationships with Spanish Art Group III. The art of the older series closely recalls that on the stone at Clonfinlough (Athlone), Ireland. The newer series in Galicia is far more developed than the older; it must probably be referred to the full Bronze Age. Some semi-naturalistic figures of animals are occasionally found.

But Peña Tú is not alone in supplying us with a clue to the age of this art-group. Engravings on pots, with figures of stag and human beings in exactly the same technique as those painted on the rock shelters in South Spain, have been found at Las Millares, at Velez Blanco itself and at Ciempozuelos near Madrid (Plate 25, nos. 1, 2, 3)(11), where these pots can be definitely assigned to the full Copper Age of the Spanish Peninsula.

Why the Copper Age folk took such trouble in decorating certain natural rock shelters, is difficult to determine. That they were not "homes" is proved by the fact that examples occur in rock shelters and situations where nobody could possibly have lived. Broadly speaking, though not invariably, the more important sites command a very extensive view and are often found near springs of fresh water. In one case at Gabal near Velez Blanco, where a rock shelter probably was used as a home, the paintings are not in the rock shelter itself, but in a niche above the doorway extremely difficult to get at, and a somewhat similar state of affairs is also known elsewhere. Possibly they were not all drawn for the same purpose, and in some cases they may have been a magic protection for the home, in others the decoration of some very visible spot that for various reasons had become a sacred sanctuary and where perhaps religious observances took place.

Another very interesting group of rock drawings occurs in the Maritime Alps not far from San Dalmazo[12] on the modern frontier between Italy and France. They are found on the slopes of and near by Monte Bego, which mountain and the Grand Capulet form two very striking peaks visible from the railway between Nice and Antibes. Col di Tenda, at the head of the Roja valley, was probably used from the very earliest times by people passing from the sea coast area of the district around Ventimiglia to the plains of Piedmont behind. Between Monte Bego and Grand Capulet lie the lakes of "wonders," and it is near these that many of the engravings in question occur. The figures drawn include bulls with very exaggerated horns, other horned animals, men, possibly villages, spirals, geometric patterns, and weapons, such as small triangular daggers with tongues, etc. (Plate 28, Fig. 1). Ploughing scenes are also depicted, there being two, more rarely four, oxen yoked, and sometimes one, sometimes two men hold the other end of the plough. Their date would seem to be some time at the beginning of the Metal period; whether Bronze was known and in use for tool-making is uncertain. The technique is a shallow pecking out of the surface of the figure, probably with a sharp stone chisel or pointed tool. But the peculiarity of this so-called Fontanalba art-group is that all the drawings are made as if seen from above; they are, as it were, aeroplane pictures of what is going on down below. Thus in the case of what seem to be drawings of villages we just find the plan of a house with the open court yard and the surrounding wall, but no elevation. The makers of these drawings apparently watched what was going on far below them and then just engraved what they had seen. Why they should have done so is a complete mystery. The plough scenes are of particular interest, the only engravings at all analogous being a plough scene, also with oxen, from the Bronze Age Scandinavian group in Bohuslain(13), a district lying to the north of Gothenburg (Sweden), where drawings of ships, men, weapons and signs occur in the greatest profusion and a ploughing scene and a cavalry battle are also depicted. More than 500 sites, where these drawings occur, have been discovered. They date to the Bronze Age and, although the motive for their creation is unknown, it is obvious when the hard nature of the glacier-worn rock surfaces on which they are carved is taken into account that a very considerable amount of work was expended in their production. This art-group had a fairly wide distribution in Scandinavia and an "outlier" of it has been found in North Russia on the eastern shore of Lake Oñega(14).

ART ON AND IN TOMBS

Not infrequently we find very rough drawings on menhirs and other upright stones. These are mostly geometric though sometimes what are probably meant to be human beings, conventionalised into sort of cross-shaped figures, and rough figures of animals, have been noted. A good example is a small kist tomb near

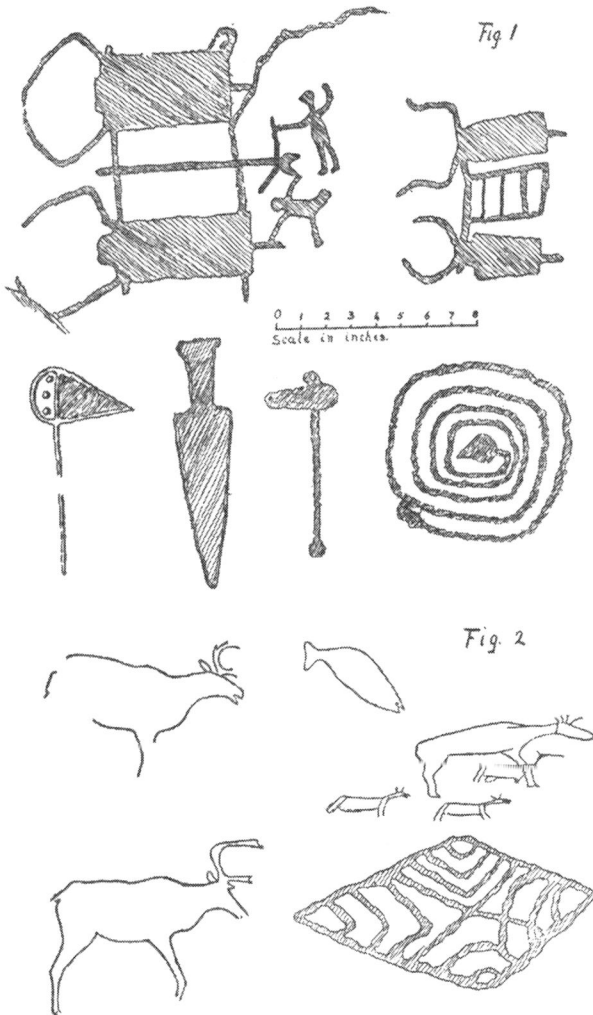

Plate 28. Fig. 1. Rock carvings from the Maritime Alps of Early Metal Age.
  „   Fig. 2. Rock carvings from Norway belonging probably to the
       "Arctic" culture.

Göhlitsch (Saxony)(15) where the representation of an axe as well as a complicated zigzag pattern is engraved on each stone. Other engravings on dolmens have been found in France and elsewhere. Some of the most elaborate examples of this style of art are found near Carnac in Brittany(16) and comprise complicated figures whose exact significance has not been determined, with any certainty, although waving corn in some instances, and the octopus in others, have been suggested. Representations of serpents have been noted, and these have been found in conjunction with polished stone axes. But in one instance at any rate, at Gavr'inis, in Brittany, the walls of a little passage grave have been covered with concentric circles and spiral decoration (Plate 29, no. 1), evidently showing connection with a different art-group, probably of Early Metal Age, that had its focus in Ireland.

The Irish examples, some apparently Late Neolithic, others as late as the Bronze Age, are restricted to an area bounded by imaginary lines drawn from Dublin, through Monaghan to Sligo, and thence to Athlone and back to Dublin(7). The most important stations are the great tumulus at Dowth, that of New Grange and a number of small tumuli on the Loughcrew hills (Co. Meath). Another example of extreme interest, as the decoration is very similar to that at Gavr'inis (Plate 29, no. 1) is found in a partially destroyed tumulus at Sess Kilgreen (Co. Tyrone) (Plate 29, no. 2), as well as on a single small standing stone near by. Again, the chamber under a now destroyed tumulus occupying a commanding position at the top of a hill, Knockmany (Co. Tyrone) was decorated in a similar manner. Of perhaps rather earlier date than the above monuments and possibly of true, though very late, Irish

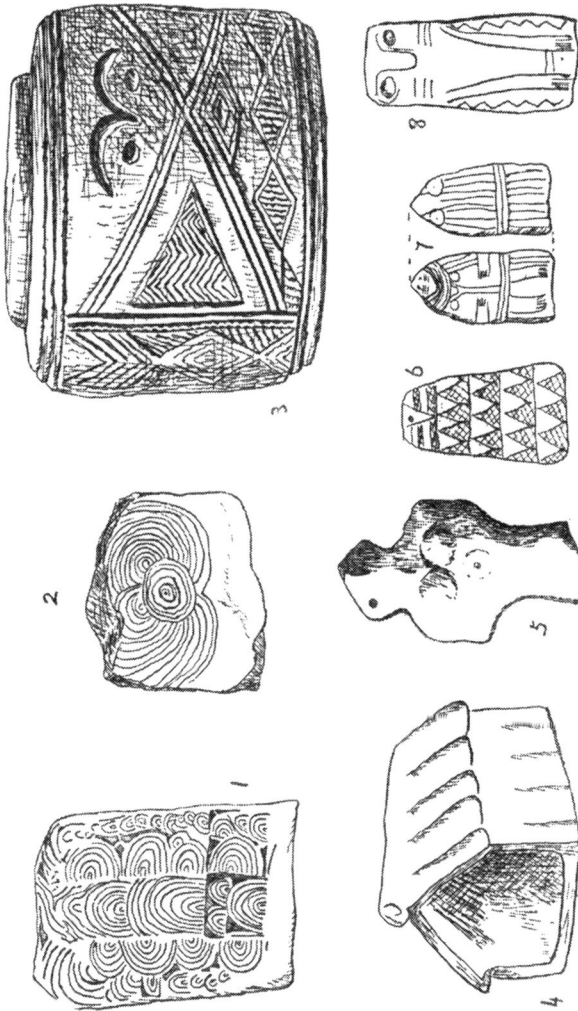

Plate 29. Carvings on the side wall of a megalithic tomb at Gavr'inis (Brittany). 2. Carvings on the side wall of a small tumulus at Sess Kilgreen (Ireland). 3. Conventionalised engravings on the Folkton chalk drum (reproduced by permission of the Trustees of the British Museum). 4. Pottery model of a house of Neolithic Age, now in the Museum at Brno. 5. Pottery figure from Anau. 6–8. "Schist" and "Menhir" idols.

Neolithic times—in all probability contemporary with the Copper Age of the Spanish Peninsula—are the engravings on the lid of a small dolmen, at Rathkenny (Co. Meath), and others on the surface of a natural slope of rock in the field behind the church at Clonfinlough (Kings Co.) (Plate 27, no. 2) not far from Athlone. The engravings at this latter site, with their peculiarities and conventionalisation, recall strongly similar conventionalisations in the Spanish Art Group III already described, and the stone at Clonfinlough is not at all unlike the earlier series of rock engravings in Galicia which have already been mentioned. The connection with Spain is not to be wondered at, for right through Early Metal Age times Ireland was of very great importance on account of the gold found there. At a rather later date the tumulus engravings developed, and, as has been seen, spread as far as Brittany.

These are not all of the same age, and four distinct methods of manufacture or technique have been noted: first and earliest, plain incised lines; secondly, pocked lines; thirdly, broad deep lines made by first pocking and then polishing and smoothing; fourth and lastly, figures pocked over the whole surface and not simply outlined. Superposition has been observed; and (1) and (2) are clearly older than the construction of the great tumuli themselves: the engravings disappear into the wall itself. In other words, the builders of the tumuli utilised stones that had already, in some instances, been engraved. It may also be observed that in some cases figures are contracted so as to fit into spaces where other and earlier techniques occur. This shows (*a*) that the engravings of the other technique are earlier, and (*b*) that the later people recognised and respected them. The significance of the art, of course,

Plate 30. Examples of the paintings of the Spanish Art Group III. Note the various conventionalisations of the human form.

is unknown. The figures consist of spirals, lozenges, zigzags, star-shaped figures, circles, the famous boat-shaped figure (New Grange), and possibly convention-alised human faces (Knockmany). In one instance, at Loughcrew, on a surface painted red a narrow zigzag is left unpainted.

The connections of this group with those elsewhere are not easy to determine, it is difficult to trace any connection with the Bronze Age art of Bohuslain in Scandinavia with its rock carvings of ships, men using a plough drawn by bulls, and a cavalry battle scene. Turning southward to Spain we may note cruciform human figures on the left hand wall of the great passage grave of Cueva Menga which may have been a later addition, although the patina of the engravings is the same as that of the rock around. There are some poor paintings in red (18) in dolmens in the provinces of Beira and Tras-os-Montes, the north of Portugal, as well as a head stone in a little dolmen under the disused church of Cangas d'Onis(19). In this latter the painting consists of wavy bands of reddish colour.

One of the most interesting art manifestations in the Spanish Peninsula is seen in the so-called schist idols (Plate 29, nos. 6 and 8) that represent the human form in a very conventionalised manner, and are roughly triangular in shape and covered with engravings (Plate 29, no. 6). These are found buried in dolmens both in Spain and Portugal; they are very common, for example, in the great tumulus field near Pavia, to the south-east of Portugal(20). They, together with "idols" made from phalange bones, etc., form a very interesting series of objects which are doubtless of ritual significance, and should in all probability be considered in connec-tion with the terra-cotta human figures that occur at

the end of Neolithic times, especially in the Eastern
Area, and appear to be connected with the general
worship of the great Earth Mother in the Near East.
In this connection may be mentioned the so-called
Menhir Idol (Plate 29, no. 7) of which several examples
have been found in France. The most characteristic
are those of Saint-Sernin, Arribats, and Pousthomy.
They represent a conventionalised human form, the
nose and eyes as well as the legs and arms being carved
in relief. A close relationship doubtless exists between
these carved grave stones and the small schist idols of
the dolmen funeral furniture and M. Pottier has also
discussed their relationship with Ethiopian megalith
monoliths [1]. It would seem probable that we are
dealing with influences from the eastern Mediterranean. A find of three small solid chalk drums engraved
all over with geometrical designs and the human face
conventionalised (see Plate 29, no. 3) found in a barrow
at Folkton Wold (Yorkshire) is of especial interest [2].
The barrow, which is 54 feet in diameter, covered a
chamber containing two adult skeletons and a beaker.
The drums were not found actually in the chamber
itself, but in a trench 22 feet away eastwards. They
date presumably to the Copper Age or perhaps Bronze
Age and should be compared with the Menhir Idols
just described.

BIBLIOGRAPHY and REFERENCES

(1) G. Hallström. "Nordskandinaviska Hällristningar." Fornvännen,
         1907 and 1908.
         —— "Hällristningar i norra Skandinavien." Ymer, 1907.
(2) F. Sarasin. "Note sur une gravure préhistorique provenant des
         tourbières de l'ancien lac de Wauwil (Lucerne)." Archiv.
         Suisses d'Anth. générale, tome ii, no. 3 (1917).

(3) See bibliography (10) at end of chapter v.

(4) See bibliography (3) at end of chapter viii.

(5) M. C. Burkitt. *Prehistory.* 2nd ed. (1925), p. 290.
—— "Spanish rock-shelter paintings of Aeneolithic Age (Spanish Group III)." *Antiq. Journ.* vol. iv, no. 2, 1924.

(6) H. Breuil. "La vallée peinte des Batuecas." *L'Anthropologie,* tome xxix, 1918–19.

(7) H. Breuil. "Le char et le traîneau dans l'art rupestre d'Estrémadure." *Terra Portuguesa,* nos. 15 and 16 (1917).

(8) H. Breuil and H. Obermaier. *La Pileta.* Monaco, 1915.

(9) E. H. Pacheco. "Las Pinturas prehistoricas de Peña Tú." *Mem. comm. de invest. pal. y prehist.* num. 2, 1914.

(10) H. Obermaier. "Die Bronzezeitlichen Felsgravierungen von Nordwest-Spanien (Galicien)." *I.P.E.K.* Leipzig, 1925.

(11) H. Obermaier. "Yacimiento prehistorico de las Carolinas (Madrid)." *Mem. comm. de invest. pal. y prehist.* num. 16, 1917.

(12) C. Bicknell. *A Guide to the Prehistoric Rock Engravings in the Italian Maritime Alps.* Bordighera, 1913.

(13) L. Baltzer. *Glyphes des Rochers du Bohuslän.* Göteborg, 1881.

(14) M. C. Burkitt. *Prehistory.* 2nd ed. Plates XLIII–XLVII.

(15) A photograph of the engraved stones is reproduced on p. 115 in vol. ii of *Human Origins,* by G. G. MacCurdy, 1924.

(16) Z. le Rouzic. *Carnac, Menhirs-statues avec signes figuratifs et amulettes ou idoles des Dolmens du Morbihan.* Nantes, 1913.
—— *Locmariaquer, la Table des Marchands.* Nancy, 1910.

(17) H. Breuil. "Les Pétroglyphes d'Irlande." *Rev. Arch.* tome xiii, pp. 75–78 (1921).
R. A. S. Macalister (with H. Breuil). "A study of the Chronology of Bronze-Age Sculptures in Ireland." *Proc. Roy. Irish Acad.* vol. xxxvi, sect. c (1921).

(18) J. L. de Vasconcellos. "Peintures dans des Dolmens de Portugal." *L'Homme préhistorique,* February 1907.

(19) Conde de la Vega del Sella. "El Dolmen de la capilla de Santa Cruz (Asturias)." *Mem. comm. de invest. pal. y prehist.* num. 22 (1919).

(20) See bibliography (1) at end of chapter vi.

(21) See *L'Illustration,* 30 May, 1925.

(22) See *British Museum Guide to the Antiquities of the Bronze Age.* 2nd ed. p. 80.

INDEX

CPSIA information can be obtained at www.ICGtesting.com
Printed in the USA
BVOW010930161211

278530BV00001B/28/P